ADVANCE PRAISE

"With this book, Fiona Williams explains more valuable information about how the mind works than you will find almost anywhere else. This enables the reader to choose the Right Mind, where the Holy Spirit dwells, instead of the wrong mind, which is mired in the ego. I was especially struck by her ability to stick to the uncompromising approach and practice of the modern spiritual classic, *A Course in Miracles*. Whether you're a student of the Course or not, I think you'll find this book to be truly helpful in your spiritual awakening." — GARY R. RENARD, best-selling author of *The Disappearance of the Universe* trilogy and *The Lifetimes When Jesus and Buddha Knew Each Other*

"I'm excited to recommend this eye-opening book, which I am certain will inspire people to step into their power through learning how to use the mind properly, which includes the practice of True Forgiveness. Fiona brilliantly explains the true cause/effect relationship in a way that will help the reader let go of victim-minded thinking. I enjoyed the personal stories, which helps one to apply the principles in their everyday life. Furthermore, Fiona takes very advanced concepts as discussed in the *A Course in Miracles* and relays them in a way that a beginner could understand. You will feel more empowered and excited to stay vigilant in your practice, and choose the Holy Spirit over the ego after reading this book!" — CINDY LORA-RENARD, best-selling Author of *A Course in Health and Well-Being* and *The Business of Forgiveness*

"As a long-time teacher of the Course, I know it as a profound, transformative spiritual pathway, but it's often dense and confusing. Using pragmatic, everyday language, Fiona brings crystal clarity to a central concept of the Course: Right-Mindedness. A gift from her mind and heart, this is the book that I wish I had 35 years ago, when I first encountered the Course." — GREGG UNTERBERGER, M.Ed., LPC, Psychotherapist, International Presenter for the Association for Research & Enlightenment, and author of *The Quickening: Leaping Ahead on Your Spiritual Journey*

AWAKENING

your *Right Mind*

Healing from fear and following
spirit with A Course in Miracles

FIONA WILLIAMS

CALL TO MIND BOOKS
CALGARY · CANADA

AWAKENING YOUR RIGHT MIND

*Healing from Fear and Following Spirit
with A Course in Miracles*

CALL TO MIND BOOKS
Calgary, Canada

www.fionamaria.ca

© Copyright 2021 by
Fiona Williams

ISBN: 978-0-9950415-5-4

COVER DESIGN:
Tamara Hackett • Sweet Clover Studios
www.sweetcloverstudios.com

INTERIOR DESIGN & TYPOGRAPHY:
D. Patrick Miller • Fearless Literary
www.fearlessbooks.com

All Course quotes are from *A Course in Miracles,*
copyright ©1992, 1999, 2007 by the Foundation for Inner Peace,
448 Ignacio Blvd. #306, Novato, CA 94949, *www.acim.org.*

References from the Combined 3rd Edition of ACIM are signified as follows:

    T-# = Text + Chapter Number
    Roman numerals = Section
    First Number = Paragraph
    Second Number(s) = sentence(s)
    W = Workbook
    pII = Part 2

CONTENTS

To my beloved husband, Eric.
Thank you for experiencing this life with me.

Preface

As a child, I witnessed the daily struggles associated with Post-Traumatic Stress Disorder which my parents both had from living through the war in Belfast, Northern Ireland known as 'the Troubles.' My mother was Catholic and my father was Protestant and their union represented treason to some on both sides. To me, a spiritual teacher, their relationship has always seemed to be the perfect example of how love shows no boundaries. Despite the danger of their coupling, they persevered and eventually immigrated to Canada in the seventies, escaping 'the Troubles' with my twin sisters, toddlers at the time.

My parents began their new life in Calgary, Alberta, a province of Canada, and had their remaining three kids, with me as their last *"whoops"* or bonus baby, as my mother calls me. Along with their trauma, I also witnessed their strength. My mother in particular would read spiritual books to help herself let go of the painful past. *A Course in Miracles* and *The Power of Now* by Eckhart Tolle being her favourites. As a child, I would borrow her books and enjoyed reading the works of Edgar Cayce and Ruth Montgomery. They opened my eyes to the spiritual realm.

One day, when I was 16 years old, I came across a familiar sight; my mother's copy of ACIM. Its beautiful navy cover with gold writing always caught my eye but this day was different. I came across the first lesson: "*Nothing I see in this room (on this street, from this window, in this place) means anything.*" I didn't quite know what to make of these words, so I closed the book and walked away unaware of how much it would eventually mean to me.

A year later, when I was 17, I began working at the church I had attended since I was a toddler, Holy Spirit Catholic Church. I was a secretary and had a couple of shifts weekly. One of those shifts was on Tuesday evenings, and my job was to ensure that the phone was answered and keep an eye on the library. Saturdays were much busier with the normal activity of a well-attended church, but I personally preferred the solitude of the Tuesday night shift.

I would frequently ignore the one major obligation of that job — never to leave the desk so I could always be there to answer the phone — and go stand in the grand and darkened foyer to stare into the eyes of the sculptures of Jesus and Mary. I would fight the initial sense of eeriness that came from the darkness and the cloaked sculptures, as I couldn't help but feel a pull to go and be with them. As I would stare into the eyes of the stunning sculptures, I would say with a sense of desperation and even urgency; "What do you know? Please tell me. Tell me." I had a deep sense that something was missing from my Catholic teachings and I was itching to find out what that was.

In my early twenties, the Course came back into my life and this time I understood it, thanks to the teachings in Gary Renard's book *The Disappearance of the Universe*. I had a deep sense of familiarity when reading the Course's words this time around. At 28, I began teaching the Course out of my home and local bookstore. A couple of years before I had left my cushy oil company job to work with my mentor, Dr. Tim Hall. Tim had recently retired from being the Vice President of the Alberta Children's Hospital and was now creating his own life coaching and self-hypnosis program. Through his years of working in psychiatric facilities across North America, Tim noticed that the power of the mind was being neglected and he aimed to change that.

My work with Tim and my ACIM studies highlighted for me the importance of the mind. I wondered how it could be so overlooked or diminished in our society when it was so obvious to me that our minds are both the creators of our world and also the perceivers. One day in 2015, I was reading through the Course and part of a sentence stood out for me: "... this is a fundamental law of the mind." Tim had introduced me to the fundamentals of the subconscious mind, which he also called 'laws', and the Course was using the same term. It excited me so I immediately grabbed my copy of the *Concordance of A Course in Miracles* and found all the places where 'law' or 'laws' was mentioned. After an hour, I had a list of sentence fragments, all referring to the ways in which our minds function.

I was excited and couldn't wait to share them, and did so in my first children's book *My Mind Book* published in 2016. This book is the adult version of *My Mind Book* and shares not only the laws of the mind but also a description of the differing minds we seem to use in this physical experience. The wrong mind of the ego, the Right Mind of Spirit, and the One Mind of Source are all covered along with the differing levels of the mind: the conscious, subconscious and unconscious minds.

What I want to help you understand is that your physical experience here is made unnecessarily harder when you use the wrong mind of the ego. You have a choice. Alternatively, you could use your Right Mind to access your Higher, Spiritual Self. All the support and comfort you have sought outside yourself actually comes from within you, through your Right Mind. Inspired (in-Spirit) thoughts are available to you and await your decision to think apart from the small and conflicted ego mind.

Your lessons in this life were not meant to punish or set you back, as the ego often implies. Your lessons have always been opportunities for you to learn that you are not the ego mind but instead the formless, powerful, and loving Mind/Spirit. You are an essential part of the One Mind of Source and your experiences here in this physical realm are meant to help you *remember* this fundamental truth. I will share some of my experiences where I used my Right Mind as my guide. I hope they will show you that you too can use your mind to benefit yourself.

The mind is often misunderstood or mislabeled as an enemy, something that "gets out of control" and must be drugged to function without harm to our general well-being. If we look at the state of mental health in our society, it is clear to see that we can no longer afford to view the mind as a dangerous force, or as impotent. It is taught in the Course that the mind never sleeps and it is always creating. You are always using it whether you are aware of it or not. Through this book, I will focus on ACIM teachings that will help you understand why and how you have been misusing your mind. I will also be sharing with you how to correct your thinking and activate your loving

Right Mind. You will learn that you no longer have to let fear thoughts or responses dominate you. You can correct them, and this is how fear will become less potent until it ultimately becomes nothing to you. Yes, this is not only possible, but wonderfully inevitable.

This experience is your path to enlightenment. Whether you are committed to enlightenment like I am, or simply wanting to have a more peaceful daily experience and calmer mind, these teachings will help you. The laws of the mind are always at work, but you can arrive at diametrically opposed results depending on which mind you are using to apply those laws. It is because you are always using them, whether you know it or not, that I strongly feel you deserve to know the laws and become aware of how you have probably been using your mind as a weapon against yourself.

You may find at times that I repeat a teaching. That is always on purpose. The ego mind can get loud and try to distract you, especially when it feels threatened, so it's helpful to repeat Right-Minded ideas so that a teaching sinks in underneath the screeching ego. This book is heavily focused on *A Course in Miracles*, so please be aware that I use terms like 'Jesus', 'Holy Spirit' and 'God' in its context. If you're put off by such terms, keep in mind that outdated definitions of these energies is an ego trick to keep conflict alive in your mind. I will share with you how these terms have been grossly misunderstood so you can hopefully welcome a new and healthy understanding of these spiritual forces. Also, any capitalizations on terms like "Who," "Right Mind," "God Mind" and the like are made to let you know when I'm referring to the higher, spiritual realm.

These teachings have helped me heal from Meniere's

disease and supported me through Caregiver's PTSD among other trials. They work because your mind is powerful and used correctly, brings you unfathomable blessings.

Before you delve in, all I can say is: you deserve the constant experience of inner peace.

Love,

Fiona

Introduction

"... think of a fountain: the mind is the engine that drives
the fountain, and spirit is the water that flows through it."
~ Kenneth Wapnick, *Journey Through the Manual of*
A Course in Miracles

I VIEW the mind as like the core of the earth, an inner center
of enormous energy whose purpose is to fuel the planet's
functioning. The mind powers our creativity and, as ACIM
philosopher Ken Wapnick suggests, serves as the activating
agent of Spirit, our True Identity. Beyond our everyday world
of form, there is the realm of Spirit where your Mind is perfectly peaceful, loving, and firmly connected with our one Source.

In daily physical experience, however, your mind probably
seems to be something different. In this world, seemingly di-
vorced from the realm of Spirit, your experience of the mind
may seem chaotic. Rather than reminding you of the universal
connection to Spirit, your mind may seem obsessed with painful memories, unhappy perceptions, and an endless stream of
trivialities. Yet hating the state of your own mind is not the
way out of your pain, conflict, or fear. It is essential to inner
healing that you appreciate the power of the mind to create
suffering, so you can learn to use it for a better purpose.

Instead of running away from your mind, something which
is impossible to do, it can be helpful to consider the possibility

that you have been using your mind incorrectly. Like any tool which has been created with positive intention for a specific purpose, misusing the mind can cause everything to go awry. A kitchen knife is an essential tool for food preparation; used as a weapon, the same knife can have tragic effects. Everyone walking this earth has used their own mind against themselves, all the while feeling like victims. It is vital to understand how you have been using your own mind as a weapon against yourself and others.

You have been distracted from the truth of your Spiritual Identity by the aimless wanderings of a tiny part of your mind. It is by recognizing and gently correcting your habitual errors of thought that you will be reintroduced to the remainder of your Mind – which knows that you are an integral part of Spirit. Despite what you may think of yourself right now, you are everything, and you deserve to know that this is true.

To comprehend that we are the ones feeding our own pain simply by misusing our minds can be sobering. Investing in negative thinking leads to an enormous amount of inner discomfort, which we will tend to project onto others so we can be rid of it, if only for a moment. Yet, with each projection, our mental anguish only strengthens in the mind and manifests in daily life melodrama, conflict, defensiveness and fear. Everyone in this physical world is dealing with this unhealthy relationship with their minds to some extent. Some may handle their thoughts better than others, but no one escapes fear thoughts entirely. As we all experience a chatty mind and a seemingly endless stream of nuisance thoughts, we are tempted to cope by attempting to shoo them away like you would a rambunctious child playing in a room filled with Grandma's precious knickknacks. *"Out! Out! Out! Away with you! Go find somewhere else to play!"*

This doesn't have to be how *you* continue to use *your* mind. No longer do you need to feed into destructive thoughts and ideas that strip you of the awareness of your True Identity. This truth is on the horizon of your unconscious mind, tucked behind some dark fearful clouds of thought you have mistakenly clung to. The truth patiently waits for you to turn your mind's powerful focus upon it. The bigger truth of Who you are is **in** your mind... are you ready to remember it?

The Choice

There is a reason why your True Identity has eluded you so far. We tend not to recognize that fear-based thinking doesn't just come upon us, but is actually our choice. You can make a decision to release yourself from the fear by not taking the thought process seriously. The decision to believe in fear, or not, is the choice you have available to you every moment throughout each day.

The teachings in this book delve deep into this ever-present choice and reveals *why* we choose fear (in any form including like anxiety, sadness, anger), and how we can become confident enough to choose peace instead. You will learn the laws of your mind's functioning, and how you can use these laws either against yourself or to benefit yourself. I will also share how fear slyly may show up in your thinking, affecting how you perceive all the people and situations you encounter throughout your daily life.

"I rule my mind, which I alone must rule."
~ A COURSE IN MIRACLES ~ Lesson 236

I will consistently emphasize that you are the gatekeeper to your own mind, always deciding upon which thoughts you would like to believe or not. By acknowledging that you are the one who is responsible for what you choose to take seriously, you step out of a victim-based mentality. No one else is in control of your mind – it's all you. Taking responsibility for your mind is an essential first step to improving your mental state. Your acceptance of the gatekeeper role will ultimately bring you to the full awareness of your True Identity as Spirit.

I will also be reinforcing and elaborating upon five major points of caring for your mind:

1. **Understanding the Cause**: Your mind is both the creator and the perceiver of your physical experience. It is through your mind which you either *create* (an expression of love) or *miscreate* (an aspect of fear) your world. As a perceiver, your mind takes in all that you see in the world through the filter of the dominant thoughts you have cemented in your mind as true. If your mind is dominated by fear thoughts, then you will allow fear to cycle through your mind via a process of projection and perception. If your mind is being used correctly, you will instead extend love to others and use Spirit's loving True Perception. Through using True Perception you can gently dissociate from the fear, guilt and pain of this physical world.

2. **Your mind is immensely powerful.** The only reason you may not believe this is that presently, deep down, you do not trust yourself. To manage our unconscious distrust of ourselves, we attempt to downplay or blatantly ignore our mind's power instead of taking responsibility for

the thoughts we invest in. We can easily get caught up in blaming our history, the people in our lives, and the current challenges we face for the condition of our mind. Although we are heavily influenced by our life's circumstances as we grow, at some point we need to take responsibility for the thoughts we choose to hold onto. Taking responsibility for our unproductive thoughts is the first step in undoing them. In order to experience true healing and genuine inner peace, it is helpful to be open to the idea that you are more powerful than you are presently aware of.

3. **You do not guard your thoughts carefully enough**. As the Course says, *"You are much too tolerant of mind wandering and you are passively condoning your mind's miscreations."* [T.2.v1.4:6] Mismanaging your fear-based thoughts leads you to strengthening them instead of recovering and ultimately healing from them. If you're honest, fear is what ultimately guides your day-to-day life and your decision making. Yet this can change and that is a choice which is always up to you.

4. **There is a healthy way out of fear and guilt, as well as the pain caused by these thought patterns**. As you are the gatekeeper to your mind, you deserve to know that there is a better way available for you to think and therefore experience your life. It is your fundamental right to be aware of this better way to use your mind!

5. **Spirit is a natural part of you**. It is taught in *A Course in Miracles* that *Spirit is in you, in a very literal way.* We are all living cases of mistaken identity as long as we think that we are separate, vulnerable, conflicted, and powerless beings. This is not the truth. Through correct

use of your mind, your True Spiritual Identity will come to the forefront of your awareness, connecting you to your inner peace, joy, and ultimate happiness. It is through the part of your mind which is connected to Spirit that you will come to be enlightened. You are so much more of love than what you seem.

The Two Parts of the Mind

Outside the realm of the One Mind of Source, commonly referred to as Heaven or Nirvana, there is the experience of consciousness and physicality. Within this lower level, the mind seems to be split into the wrong mind of the ego and the Right Mind of Spirit. It is through our use of the ego mind that we get the "foe" experience, where the mind seems to be working against us as it replays scripts of conflict and pain. The Right Mind is the part connected to Spirit, and from there we receive Spirit's loving guidance commonly known as *inspiration* (in-spirit). Therefore, using our Right Mind *is* the path to enlightenment.

You are the "decision maker" and can become a gentle observer who takes a step back from the battle of the wrong mind and sees clearly the choice between fear and peace. When we accept this definition of the mind, we can see why there is a part of our minds, the ego mind, with which we want nothing to do with. As you learn more about the ego mind, you will see why you have wanted to shoo your mind away, cover it up and diminish its role in your life.

You can learn to use your Right Mind consistently so that you gently dissociate from the ego mind. Regardless of the battles that may preoccupy your daily mind, the first step to peace is to recognize that your mind is something which simply needs your care and attention. From that recognition, you can step forward to know the profound aspect of your Mind that will show you the way Home. I hope this book provides some helpful 'travel tips' for that journey.

CHAPTER ONE

The Wrong Mind

WHEN you give a thought your attention, you are giving it your mind's immense power. From the moment you notice a thought, you've latched on to it and now face the choice of watching it grow or letting it go. When identified solely with the ego mind, we will choose to let many fearful thoughts grow. Constant misuse of the mind in this way creates a mental holding pattern where everything is eerily the same as you repeat your ego stories.

All thoughts affect our neural pathways, which I liken to paths in a field of grass. Trodden upon once, the grass is momentarily squished. Day after day of following the same path, the grass gets firmly pressed down. As you continue to use the path, the grass disappears, the soil is exposed and eventually becomes compressed while along the sides grows tall. You dare not step to the side of the path and disturb the long grass for you don't know what lingers there. You just stick to the old and familiar path. Once trodden upon, it is easier to go down again and again. It is the path of least resistance, or *habit*.

But habits can be broken before they break us. The ego mind resides mostly in the unconscious, fueling and flavoring your waking, conscious experience. You are only aware of some of it, yet it creeps up all the time and regularly influences your actions. You can, with sincere commitment and practice, undo the ego in your mind with the help of Spirit. That means you choose to follow a new path and bring about a more loving state of mind.

About the ego

Negative thoughts seem to pop out of nowhere, often with such regularity that they may haunt you. Perhaps you find that you can't let a bitter judgment or a hurtful comment go. These are what my sisters and I like to call "sticky thoughts." By their nature, such ego thoughts are repetitive, aimless, and negative.

When you think only with the ego mind you will find your thoughts swirling in a vortex of memories, fantasies of conflict, and general chaos that can cause both mental and physical pain. In the Course we are taught that the ego was made out of fear and therefore knows not of love. That's why the ego is incapable of loving you or even liking you; it simply doesn't know how because it is the antithesis of love.

In our world, thinking with the ego mind and acting upon its decisions is considered normal. The ego's ways of thinking are preoccupied with judgment, always seeking to divide people from each other through comparison and condemnation. If you watch the frequency of judgments on social media, you can see how these ways of thinking are valued in our society. Thinking with the ego may seem to offer a feeling of supremacy over others. This feeling of superiority leads to an addiction in ego-driven thinking, and genuine inner peace seems to elude us merely because we believe that the ego's ways are just "the way things are." Without questioning the ego's functioning we stay stuck in it, perpetuating conflict within and without.

Thinking with the ego-mind seems normal because of two unconscious assumptions:

1. You made the ego and so you are loyal to what you made.
2. You believe you actually are the ego.

This is why fearful, conflicted thoughts stream through your mind with such unrelenting force. Negative thoughts are not something being done to you, they are being done by you. In my early twenties I was going through a particularly strong bout of anxiety, and I knew that I was doing it to myself. I knew that my mind was untrained and I was the one who would have to learn to calm my mind. This realization helped take the sting out of the anxious thoughts and I would sometimes shake loose from them by singing these lyrics to the song, "Just" by Radiohead: *"You do it to yourself, you do. And that's what really hurts. Is that you do it to yourself, just you. You and no one else. You do it to yourself."*

Your only way out of a hellish thought system is to understand why you believe and invest in the ego's dictates. Before we dive deep into the ego's thought system and expose it, please remember that just as you made the ego, you can change your mind about it. This is your key to peace. As the error of the ego is made in your mind, it is also corrected in your mind.

"The key to salvation is but this, I am doing this unto myself." ~ T.27.VIII.10:1

What is the ego?

There are many names for the ego: the false self, the small self, the monkey mind. The term *ego* is just shorthand for *the thought system of fear*. In ACIM the ego is referred to as the wrong mind, a part of our self-awareness that went rogue: *"The ego is a confusion in identification."* ~ T.7.VIII.4:7

Personally, I like to refer to the ego as a mis-thought in itself. It is not some snarling beast coming at us from the depths of a fiery chasm, nor is it untamable. The ego is simply a mistake that can be corrected. You'll be doing yourself a favour to stop being afraid of this part of your mind, instead regarding it neutrally. Like a storm cloud passing over, the ego won't last. If you stop feeding the ego with your belief in it, its thoughts will pass by more quickly.

How did the ego come to be?

The birth of the ego was a tiny, mad idea suggesting we could be apart from our Source. An idea doesn't have any power unless it is taken seriously, and this insane idea was mistaken seriously by us. Without your mind's incredible power of belief, thoughts pass by and leave us unchanged. The ego is simply a bad idea, which is an idea in itself, is given life through your belief. If you didn't believe in it, the ego or any of its nonsense thoughts simply wouldn't bother you.

*"**Do not be afraid of the ego.** It depends on your mind, and as you made it by believing in it, so you can dispel it by withdrawing belief from it."* ~ T.7.VIII.5:1-2

Within the natural state of Oneness, a part of your mind seemed to fall into a state of separateness. In this instant, two things happened:

1.   The part of your mind that believes it separated from its Source fell asleep. It is now experiencing a vivid

and continuous dream where all things appear
disconnected.
2. The tiny, mad idea of the separate ego projected the
entire physical effect of the universe.

The idea of separation is commonly known as the "fall of
man," symbolically depicted as Adam and Eve being cast out
of the Garden of Eden. I have always felt though that Eckhart
Tolle described the separation best when he wrote:

> *"Humans have been in the grip of pain for eons, ever
> since they fell from the state of grace, entered the
> realm of time and mind (ego mind), and lost aware-
> ness of Being. At that point, they started to perceive
> themselves as meaningless fragments in an alien uni-
> verse, unconnected to the Source and to each other."*

From the moment of the tiny, mad idea being taken seriously, the physical universe was spawned along with the realm
of consciousness. There are some who glorify consciousness
itself as a path to enlightenment. In the Course we are taught
that *"Consciousness, the level of perception, was the first split
introduced into the mind after the separation, making the
mind a perceiver rather than a creator. Consciousness is correctly identified as the domain of the ego."* ~ T.3.IV.2:1-2

Consciousness is not what we are but what we are experiencing. It is subject to degrees and levels and a multitude of
emotions. Consciousness is where duality comes into play:
from out of oneness arises twoness and disconnection. It is
possible to progress or rise up in levels of consciousness, but it
is still not what we truly are.

Here is an illustration depicting the level of Source and the level of the physical world.

ONE MIND

SOURCE, SPIRIT, ONENESS, LOVE, GOD

SPLIT MIND

ILLUSION - DREAM STATE
PART OF MY MIND IS ASLEEP

WRONG MIND
(EGO)

- BELIVE IT
SEPARATED FROM
SOURCE
- THOUGHT SYSTEM
OF GUILT & FEAR

RIGHT MIND
(CONNECTED TO
SPIRIT)

- KNOWS YOU NEVER
LEFT SOURCE
- REMINDS YOU OF
YOUR INNOCENCE

It's important for your salvation from the ego mind that you fully acknowledge that this world is not real nor is it your Home. As this physical experience is a product of the ego mind, it is, like the ego, illusory. As mentioned, the part of your mind which thinks this physical experience is real is asleep and dreaming. In the Course, the following profound question is posed to us: How can you wake up from a dream if you don't know you're dreaming? In order to wake up to your Reality, it's essential that you recognize that you're presently asleep.

To help others grasp this incredible notion, I ask them if they've ever felt homesick. You can check in with yourself: Is there a part of you that just doesn't feel right in this world?

Like you don't belong? The Course tells us that we are aliens here, and somewhere in our minds we know this is true. The part of our minds which knows the Truth is always calling out to us. Those twinges of homesickness you may get is a part of yourself nudging at you to pay attention.

> *"The separation was not a loss of perfection, but a failure in communication." ~ T.6.IV.12:5*

How is the ego sustained?

Not only has your belief in the tiny, mad idea convinced you that you're apart from your Source; it has also told you that you are alone, vulnerable, and worst of all, guilty. It is the immense guilt over believing that you walked away from your Source which keeps you chained to the ego. Deep down you feel that your Source is livid with you for walking away from It, and so the ego, even with all its complexity and chaos, still feels safer to you than facing the supposed wrath of God. This insane idea that your Source wants to punish you is the root of all your fears. Guilt and fear are what make up the ego's thought system. There are several ways you perpetuate the ego's thought system, or mismanage guilt and fear so that they seem all-powerful.

> *"Guilt remains the only thing that hides the Father, for guilt is the attack upon His Son. The guilty always condemn, and having done so they will still condemn, linking the future to the past as is the ego's law."*
> *~ T.13.IX.1:1-2*

Belief

The ego is sustained in your mind by your belief in it. Remember, you made the ego and so you think it's real. The Course reminds us we are way too preoccupied with listening to its voice; we take everything it says seriously. This keeps your mind focused upon the details of this physical world, so that you accept its seeming reality and believe there is nothing else for you to strive towards.

Although fueled by guilt, the ego is keen on keeping you unaware of that, so you won't seek to heal it. Simply by not looking at your guilt, you sustain the ego in your own mind. To keep you unaware of your unconscious guilt, the ego frames your guilt in a multitude of different pictures. That way you're never aware that your guilt over the tiny, mad idea is your real issue. For example, if you stub your toe and feel pain, the pain you feel is actually rooted in your mind's guilt, not your toe. If someone cuts you off in traffic and you flip them off, you've retaliated because of your guilt. And in a more extreme case, someone who murders does it because of the guilt in their mind. We don't usually recognize guilt in such situations, and that's just how the ego likes it. If you don't recognize your pain, anger, and vengeance as rooted in unconscious guilt, the guilt remains safely hidden in your mind.

Judgement

Because guilt always lurks in the background of your awareness, the ego's go-to strategy for every situation is judgement. Whenever you make a judgement your perception of duality is reinforced. That's because a judgment of "good" or "bad" always harbors its polar opposite, For example, let's say you are nominated for an award. You could easily make the judgement that receiving the award would be good, but that would mean *not* receiving the award is bad. Now you have both possibilities in your mind and you are not at peace about whatever the results may be.

The Course challenges us to question the value of judging, because we tend to glorify it. Our judgements pollute our own minds and end up muddying our own perception of ourselves. While we have to make choices when ordering a cup of coffee or deciding to wear a certain outfit, we can do so neutrally if we are not driven by guilt. Should you not be able to get that cup of coffee or find the outfit you wanted, you're still at peace. Being free of the dependence on the world for our peace and happiness is the route to inner peace.

However, even simple choices can be contaminated with judgment if the sheer ignorance and arrogance of the ego are at play — especially when you make "judgement calls" about other people. We are taught in the Manual for Teachers that in order to judge someone correctly, you'd have to be aware of all things past and present. "Who except in grandiose fantasies would claim this [ability] for themselves?" asks the Course. We judge strictly from our own experiences and perceptions, and this is why we are so frequently wrong about others. Our judgements actually reflect the content of our own minds, projected out onto others.

If you did not judge anyone, your mind would be clear of thoughts and you would naturally feel peaceful. Judgement entrenches you in this world; non-judgement frees your mind from it.

Projection

Another habitual strategy of the ego is projection, a key means of avoiding guilt. Your guilt is so intense you cannot bear to feel it all. So the ego directs you to deny it is yours, then project it out into the world. Projection itself accomplishes three things for the ego:

1. It keeps you looking outside yourself so you do not find the truth of Who you really are within your own mind.

2. It convinces you that everyone and everything around you are indeed separate from you; therefore separation must be true.

3. Finally, projection keeps you in conflict because it is through projection that you blame other people or your general circumstances for your mental pain. *"Projection means anger, anger fosters assault, and assault promotes fear."* ~ T.6.I.3:3

Repetition

Lastly, the ego is sustained in your mind through the ceaseless repetition of thoughts that confirm separation. Through the ego mind we strengthen our association with this physical world and all the dramas that come with it. We analyze our issues, dissect our anxieties, tell pained stories of the past and construct fantasies about the future to ourselves and anyone who will listen. We'll look at more ways in which we repeat ego thoughts in the section on the law of the mind.

Through my years of teaching, I've seen people get overwhelmed with the seeming magnitude of the ego. It has been believed in and sustained for eons. I've found it helpful to remember that it's just a tiny part of our minds having this ego experience; the majority of our Mind knows where we really are, safe in our Source. The ego cannot survive in the light of the Truth which is also in your mind.

> *"This fragment of your mind is such a tiny part of it that, could you but appreciate the whole, you would see instantly that it is like the smallest sunbeam to the sun, or like the faintest ripple on the surface of the ocean."* ~ T.18.VIII.3:3

Remember that whenever you choose to respond to the ego seriously, you are choosing to replay the moment of the separation. You are choosing to be separate from others and at a deeper level you are choosing to be separate from your Source. In the Course, it is written that every time we choose conflict or fear in any form, we replay the tiny, mad idea. By choosing the ego, we are saying that our ego's will is more important to us than our Source's loving Will. We delude ourselves with the notion that ego is stronger than Source. This judgement will always cause some discomfort because you are choosing to go against the grain of your True Identity.

Why don't I trust myself?

When you associate with the ego mind you're going to have a hard time trusting yourself. Your belief that you were successful in carrying out the tiny, mad idea of separation is the source of your distrust in yourself and the main factor in diminishing the power of your mind. The pain and guilt over the tiny, mad idea is so intense that you don't want to face it; so, you pretend that your mind isn't powerful.

In daily life, the distrust in yourself can show up in a variety of ways: you may be afraid of saying something wrong at a party, or fear you'll make a mistake in a professional project, or expect to sabotage a romantic relationship. You may even be anxious that anxieties like these have crept into your mind. It is because you identify with the ego that you believe such thoughts, and you are left terrified.

Believing that we are flawed, or even potential perpetrators, is so painful that we may find comfort in seeing other people behave worse than we ever have. If a murderer is found guilty and will be locked up in prison for decades, we may think, *"Good! That dude deserves it. Throw away the key!"* This is an example of how the ego mind offers the delusion that someone else's failure or crime saves you from guilt.

Still, your distrust in yourself though has not prevented your mind from working at full capacity. This is why the Course is so keen on helping us to acknowledge how powerful our minds are. It's vital that we get a grip on our thinking and start using our minds correctly. It's time we start appreciating our minds and realize that every moment of every day, whether we are asleep or awake, our mind's power never ceases as it is always at work.

"Few appreciate the real power of the mind, and no one remains fully aware of it all the time. However, if you hope to spare yourself from fear there are some things you must realize, and realize fully. The mind is very powerful and never loses its creative force. It never sleeps. Every instant it is creating. It is hard to recognize that thought and belief combine into a power surge that can literally move mountains. It appears

at first glance that to believe such power about your-
self is arrogant, but that is not the real reason you do
not believe it. You prefer to believe that your thoughts
cannot exert real influence because you are actually
afraid of them. This may allay awareness of guilt,
but at the cost of perceiving the mind as impotent. If
you believe that what you think is ineffectual you may
cease to be afraid of it, but you are hardly likely to
respect it." ~ T.2.VII.9:1-12

But I don't feel guilty

I have come across some in my ACIM classes who wonder if guilt is really the issue. They don't feel guilt intensely
very often so they're unsure which is understandable. Yet, our
cluelessness over our guilt is exactly how the ego would have
it. If you wonder if guilt is really your issue you can simply reflect upon how you've felt when a cop car has pulled up behind
you at a red light. Did you start to do a mental check to remember if your car insurance and registration was valid? Did
you worry about whether or not you indicated when you last
changed lanes? Or, did you just feel uncomfortable and uncertain? That's guilt. Even though you probably drove perfectly
and your paperwork is up to date, you still have that nagging
feeling of *"Did I do something wrong?!"* Honestly, how often
does this feeling show up in your life?

This is but a taste of the immense guilt lingering in the
depths of your unconscious mind. What's happening when you
react negatively to any circumstances is that your unconscious
guilt is being triggered. Some personalities or circumstances
are more powerful triggers than others, but all deserve your lov-

ing attention so they can be corrected. I always say that guilty reactions reveal which ego-based ideas you're holding onto.

I remember when my beloved dog Guinness passed away from cancer. Two days after he died, I hopped on a plane to join my parents and a couple of my sisters on vacation in Scottsdale, Arizona where my parents had rented a condo. As my husband was working out of town that week, I didn't want to be alone and thought I would take the opportunity to be in a new environment, escaping the snowy start to spring in Calgary. I was also grateful for the opportunity to rest after six weeks of restless days and nights caring for my darling dog.

On the second evening there, I said goodnight early and went to bed. From my bed I could see my parents sitting and reading in the living room. If there was a place and time I should have felt peaceful, it was then. Yet, something peculiar was happening every time I closed my eyes to go to sleep. A vision of locking Guinness out of my house kept coming to my mind. The vision was accompanied with such a horrible visceral feeling of guilt; why would I ever think that I would cast him out of our home? Every time the vision came to my mind, my right leg would kick as a reaction to the discomfort and thrust me out of the vision. I would then open my eyes and see my parents sitting peacefully, still reading in the living room.

The vision happened six times before I finally took steps to correct my thinking and ask Spirit for help. I reflected on the core issue of the vision: casting away a beloved and locking them out of my house and life. A profound realization then came to me. I exclaimed to myself, *"Holy shit! This is what I think I did to God!"* I couldn't ignore the correlation. The guilt accompanied with the vision was so intense that it was unbearable. I was surprised that I hadn't recognized this high level of guilt within me. The guilt was there, deep in my mind, just waiting for the opportunity to surface. Clearly, my having gone through such a hard time in the weeks previous emotionally triggered the guilt in my unconscious mind.

I had to look at this guilt and heal it. There was no way around that for me. What helped me then and what may help you now is to know that our guilt over the tiny, mad idea is unfounded. Remember that the ego thought system and this experience of separation is an illusion. It's not real. It just *feels* real due to the power of our minds. It's vital that you know that your spiritual Source isn't mad at you; It sees you as innocent. Spirit knows that the tiny, mad idea was just a mistake to be corrected, not a sin to be punished. Mistakes are corrected through love and it is unconditional love which Spirit has for us. Spirit says, *"Don't worry, everything is okay. You're safe. You can wake up from the nightmare."*

Every time guilt screams at you about how horrible you are, you can practice not reacting as if it were true. This will take practice because simply you are in the habit of reacting to guilt seriously. All habits can be broken and replaced with healthy ones.

In this world there will be no shortage of opportunities to react to events or people negatively. Instead you can let your reactions be your cue to correct your thoughts and heal your guilt. Essentially, the guilt over thinking you left your Source is your number one issue. Left unchecked, this enormous guilt dictates your thoughts, your beliefs, your actions and your responses. Left unchecked, your guilt rules you.

If I don't correct my guilt
then what am I doing with it?

If you are not correcting your guilt when it shows up, then you are going to project it. But you will never get rid of the guilt through projection because the world around you is itself a projection, already running on the theme of guilt. In the Course, it is consistently reinforced that *projection makes perception*, meaning that whatever we project we will perceive in the world as real. This is how guilt is cycled through your mind.

The problem is not that ego thoughts pop into your mind; the real issue is that you give your ego thoughts your *belief*. The moment you endorse a guilty ego thought as real, projection is soon to follow. This process can be instantaneous, like suddenly "losing your temper" because someone triggers you. As the ego is undone in your mind, your endorsement of ego thoughts will become less automatic as you'll be more aware of your reactions. Without awareness of your thought patterns and your reactions to them, you will inevitably project any discomfort, compounding the guilt in your mind. This is how negative thinking snowballs.

On the next page, see an illustration showing the dynamic of how ego guilt thoughts are perpetuated:

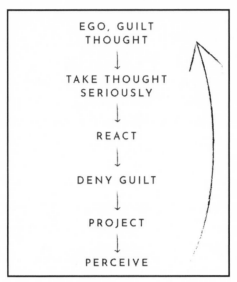

EGO, GUILT
THOUGHT

↓

TAKE THOUGHT
SERIOUSLY

↓

REACT

↓

DENY GUILT

↓

PROJECT

↓

PERCEIVE

The ego's survival relies upon your decision to disown your guilt and place the blame on others. Common statements like *"You hurt my feelings"* or *"They made me do it"* or *"You made me feel this way"* are typical expressions of projection. Not only does the ego try to make the behaviour of others the problem, it also suggests that you are powerless because other people negatively affect you without your say-so.

Projection is how you put a mask over your guilt. The mask over your guilt can look like any fear-based reaction you have to any person or situation. Some examples of disguised guilt include anger about climate change, fear of another pandemic, sadness over a failed relationship, or feeling taken advantage of by an employer. There are innumerable ways the ego can mask your guilt so you don't recognize it for what it is.

"Problems are not specific but they take specific forms, and these specific shapes make up the world. And no one understands the nature of his problem."
~ T.27.V.8:1-2

In your daily waking life, your guilt is why you feel like a victim. You feel vulnerable to the world, stealing your focus from the truth within. Beneath the victim façade, you are not actually worried about what another may do to you, but what you could do to them. Deeper in your mind you believe that you are the perpetrator.

Why do I feel powerless?

It is easy to take a look at our individual identities in this physical universe and feel small, even insignificant. Feeling this is essential to the ego's plan because it doesn't want us to realize that we are actually immensely powerful. The curious thing is that the ego, powered by our own minds, aims to tell us that we are powerless. This is the ego paradox.

"The ingeniousness of the ego to preserve itself is enormous, but it stems from the very power of the mind the ego denies. This means that the ego attacks what is preserving it, which must result in extreme anxiety... The ego draws upon the one source that is totally inimical to its existence for its existence. Fearful of perceiving the power of this source, it is forced to depreciate it." ~ T.7.VI.3:1-2/5

This paradox means that the ego's very existence depends upon a lie. In order to sustain a lie, you have to compound and elaborate on it, increasing the associated pain. This is what you have been playing into for eons — a myth designed to disempower you.

Know that the ego is afraid of you. The ego knows that at any moment you could direct the power of your mind to the truth, and then the ego would disappear. To keep you from withdrawing your belief in it, the ego is strict on the suggestion that you aren't powerful enough to do anything. Falling for its lies you end up misperceiving yourself and settling for being less than you really are. You also project this idea onto other people, seeing them as helpless victims.

The Ego's Agenda

> *"Because we are quite subtle in maintaining this mind-less state, it is essential that we understand the ego's strategy. Such understanding also helps us to recognize the ego's shyness in attempting to undermine our recognition of what it is up to."* ~ Kenneth Wapnick, *Journey Through the Text of ACIM,* Vol. 1, Chapter 8, Pg. 215.

In this section, I will cover the ego's agenda followed by its "laws" of chaos that outline the delusional beliefs of the ego's thought system. The Course suggests that when we think with the ego our minds are actually blank; the ego is devoid of meaning and therefore we are mindless whenever we think along with it. What's uncomfortable to acknowledge is how often we are in this blank, mindless state. All the ego can offer us is an endless search through this physical world for something which is not there. The Course teaches that the ego's agenda is *"...seek and do not find"* ~ T.12.IV.1:4. What we are truly looking for is our deep connection with Source — a connection in our minds, not in the world.

The physical world can offer up some nice venues and scenery that may reflect peace and feel inviting. But as anyone who has been anxious knows, a chatty, fearful mind is a powerful deterrent to peace regardless of how calming your physical environment may be. No matter where you go within this world your mind will follow you everywhere, so it's important to begin training your mind instead of letting it run wild.

Knowing the ego's agenda has helped me de-escalate my response to fear thoughts. It has also reminded me that if I choose the ego, I'm only going to get more ego. That makes the choice for healing the obvious, sane choice. In my kitchen I keep a sticky note that says, *"The desire to heal is the only sane response."* Once you begin to see that thinking with the ego leads to purely undesirable effects, you're more apt to take a step back from ego thoughts.

You know by now that the ego intends on keeping you locked in its thought system because it needs your mind and your loyalty to survive. To do this, the ego's agenda comprises three main objectives:

- Keeping you distracted from the Truth
- Keeping you in conflict
- Keeping you focused on the external world and your body

Keeping you distracted from the Truth

"The changes the ego seeks to make are not really changes. They are but deeper shadows, or perhaps different cloud patterns." ~ The Process of Psychotherapy: The Limits of Psychotherapy 2:6-7

By its very nature, the ego's style of thinking is chatty, judgmental and tangential. It's also quite loud. You may have experienced the frustration of not being able to quiet your mind for a meditation session. I've chatted with many people who actually beat themselves up for not being able to just sit for a few minutes with a peaceful mind. They tend to feel defeated. Yet, it's helpful to note that a chatty mind is not a sign of weakness; it's happening because the ego is threatened by your power. Remember: your ability to look within and connect with Spirit is death to the ego. It is therefore very loud and distracts you with nonsensical thoughts to prevent its demise.

With the ego, your mind just wanders aimlessly and you follow it along. This is how our ego minds function predominantly throughout the waking day. You may notice that your thinking hops around from topic to topic. Perhaps you can recall a time when you noticed that you started thinking about one topic, like a close friend, then ten minutes later you realize you're thinking about an old job you once had. Upon reflection, you would probably be able to retrace the stream of memories and fantasies, both good and bad, that you touched upon. This is an example of the ego's tangential style.

Being distracted by the ego is not just about your mind wandering off — which is a choice, by the way — it's also about how often you are taking the ego's ramblings seriously. By affording the ego your attention and investing in it, you are literally giving the ego your mind's incredible power to use for its own purposes. Thinking too much with the ego leads to feeling irritable, angry, or even like you've hit a wall.

Personally, I find it relieving to know why my mind can get chatty. When anxiety was beginning to rise for me in my early twenties, I found myself replaying old "Friends" episodes in my head. I'm all for a good laugh but it became quite tedious to have my mind showing repeats. And that's just what's happening when you find yourself reviewing old songs, shows or movies, even when you're replaying (or improving) conversations you've had – that's all ego.

Here is a list of symptoms of ego distraction mode:

- Analysis
- Obsessiveness
- Aimless thinking
- Songs, sentences or words stuck in your head
- Incessant inner chatter
- Replaying old conversations or situations
- Fantasizing about conflict

"An untrained mind can accomplish nothing."
~ Workbook Introduction – 1:3

Keeping you in conflict

The second aspect of the ego's agenda is to maintain the thought system of separation. One of the ways this is accomplished is through conflict. The Course tells us that the ego is at least suspicious, and at its worst it is vicious. Conflict is constant, only varying in degrees of intensity.

You may have questioned why you're so suspicious of other people, even people you've never met. Or you may have noticed that you conjure up fantasies of being in conflict with others. The suspicious nature of the ego's thinking serves the purpose of ensuring that you don't unite with others. Healing from the ego mind involves seeing us all as one and treating everyone equally. If you're in conflict with someone, you won't think of them this way. If you're unsure of someone, don't fully trust them or simply don't like them, then you're going to feel comfortable projecting onto them. This can only perpetuate conflict in your own mind and life.

Conflict in your mind is initiated through perceiving yourself as separate from others. More specifically, conflict needs the dualistic perception of a 'me' and a 'you'. From there the ego mind is able to compare. I like to say that comparison is the seed of conflict. Once you compare, conflict in some form naturally arises. Here is a description of the initiation of conflict in your mind.

Separation – Which requires duality; a 'me' and a 'you'

Comparison – The ego mind perceives differences between the 'me' and 'you'

Conflict – The differences are used as "evidence" that the other is different from you and therefore they threaten your individual persona because you are not alike.

The conflict of the ego will always involve some sort of threat; the small self which you believe you are is easily offended and often feels victimized. If you reflect upon your own thinking, you may notice how common it is that you feel you have been misjudged and misunderstood. Judgement, attack, and victimization are essentials to the ego's separation agenda. They all keep your mind fixated on conflict.

"If you did not feel guilty, you could not attack, for condemnation is the root of attack."
~ T.13.Introduction.1:1

The ego will look for anyone to play the role of antagonist in your life story. By scanning for and then highlighting any differences you have with others, the ego proceeds to use those differences as ammunition against them and ultimately, your-self. In the Course, we are taught that the ego mind focuses on our differences from others that make us special. This is why we feel so offended when our uniqueness is attacked. Even if we don't *like* what makes us unique, we still get our backs up when we are judged as ordinary or unimportant. This is be-cause our ego identity is all that we think we are. From this perspective, anyone can easily become your enemy.

The ego tells you that you are a lone wolf, and must keep an eye out for the untrustworthy person who treads upon your territory. You may not be keenly aware of this defensive stance, especially if you enjoy connecting with other people. Yet if you gently reflect upon your thinking, you may be able to see how uncertain and defensive you can be in certain environments. For example: Do you hate it when people don't give you their full attention while you're speaking? Or does it bug you when people don't reply to a text message from you right away? Per-haps you don't care for people who drive a certain way or have a different political viewpoint. All those little things which bug you about other people's behaviour are excuses the ego uses to make conflict when there doesn't need to be any. There are scores of ways the ego can set you apart from others if you let it. Habitually judging others keeps you in conflict.

Keeping you focused on the external world

Along with upholding conflict in your mind, the ego main-tains the idea of separation in your mind by focusing your at-tention on the external world, especially your body. The more you focus on the physical world, the more you will believe that you are separate from others and the world. This is also another method of distraction from the Truth, for as long as you are looking outside of yourself, you are not looking within yourself. Using the ego mind means you rely on the world and your life's circumstances to make you happy. Essentially, the ego keeps you dependent upon the world and the comfort of your body for your happiness.

The body itself is a hiding place the ego has invented to keep it safe from the supposed wrath of God. To think that all you are is a body, vulnerable to time and countless dangers, is a perception which obviously leads to a lot of fear. We spend an enormous amount of time glorifying the body, hating it, trying to control it, and generally worrying about it. Worst of all, we give our power away to the body thinking that it is at the center of our reality. By focusing on the world and the body, we forget that our minds are at the center of creation.

Considering how unpredictable the world can be, it is not a stable platform you can depend upon for your peace and joy. Relying on the world leads to insecurity, to say the least. You will attempt to control it so you don't get blindsided by its unpredictability. Deep down what you're really trying to control, though, is that your unconscious guilt doesn't get triggered by untoward events. Eckhart Tolle would refer to this as your "pain body." Regardless of how your pain body is feeling attacked, it's your unconscious guilt that makes the situation uncomfortable. The need to control your world comes from the avoidance of facing your discomfort about the tiny, mad idea.

Your attempts to control your world can show up in many ways, like managing the amount of calories you consume, being obsessed with how you look, or even trying to manage how other people speak to you. There's no peace in living like this.

As long as you are focused on controlling the world, you are too busy to quiet your mind and feel the literal peace of God which is within you.

It's important to note that there is nothing wrong with having an external environment you enjoy and a healthy relationship with your body. Yet the best route to ease in your circumstances is keeping your focus on the state of your mind. The "evidence" for separation is all around you, and your five senses attest to your separateness at all times. Yet it is your mind, not your physical eyes, which will sense your connection to all. For there will come the day where we will all lay the body and this world aside, and it is our minds that will carry on.

We've looked at the ego's agenda and what it intends to hide from you. Now, we will examine the ego's "laws" of chaos, ensuring not only that others are seen as your enemy but your Source seems like an enemy as well. As you will learn, seeing someone as your enemy is one of the most harmful things you can do to your state of mind.

The Ego's "Laws" of Chaos

The ego has its own set of "laws" to serve its agenda. Whenever you take an ego-based thought seriously, these "laws" come into play in your mind. But these are not really laws at all — they are statements of delusion. Whenever we think with the ego mind, we are delusional. The ego's "laws" were designed to keep your mind asleep, caught in the illusory dream of separation. They are intended to keep you totally unaware of love's presence within you.

Since they are without sense or meaning, you will never be able to understand these chaotic "laws." As I always say to my clients, you can't find sense in nonsense. When you think about how often we get caught up in trying to make sense out of the conflict in our lives, there's really no point to it. The ego's ways are purposely complex; the more you search within them for meaning, the more you get tangled up in its web of complexity. This is why inner peace seems so elusive. We keep playing along with the chaos required for the ego to stay alive in our minds.

Here you will learn what you are allowing to happen within your own mind when you choose to think with the ego. This is how you presently perceive your world and it's not pretty. These "laws" will highlight how you make enemies of others and also your Source. If you are the type of person who struggles with the term "God", you will learn the deeper reason as to why you feel this way in this section.

> *"The 'laws' of chaos can be brought to light, though never understood. Chaotic laws are hardly meaningful, and therefore out of reason's sphere. Yet they appear to be an obstacle to reason and to truth. Let us, then, look upon them calmly, that we may look beyond them, understanding what they are, not what they maintain. It is essential it be understood what they are for, because it is their purpose to make meaningless, and to attack the truth. Here are the laws that rule the world you made. And yet they govern nothing, and need not be broken; merely looked upon and gone beyond." ~ T.23.II.1:1-7*

"LAW" OF CHAOS #1:

The Truth is Different for Everyone

"This law maintains that each is separate and has a different set of thoughts that set him off of others."
~ T.23.II.2:2

You have already learned of the ego's need for conflict to ensure separation is upheld in your mind. In order to maintain the illusion of separateness, the ego relies upon our perceiving differences which we then use to make comparisons, which in turn leads to conflict in the mind. This first "law" of chaos or delusion sets the stage for conflict in the mind by stating that the truth is different for everyone. In our world, this first chaotic "law" is easy to observe. Differing opinions on politics, morals, or any other topic are used to distance oneself from others, and then as grounds for attack.

This first "law" of chaos sets up the idea that people are either for or against us. In the Course, this is described in terms of "special love" or "special hate" relationships. If you agree with someone then you love them. That love is completely dependent on the fact that for a little while, two persons' ideas of what is true and right in this world match up. The special love relationship can easily lead to idolatry, enabling, and co-dependency. The Course teaches that every time we raise up an idol in our minds, that idol will inevitably fall and we will weep. Special love is a very shaky foundation for any relationship.

Then there is the "special hate" relationship, the more obvious result of this first chaotic "law". This is how enemies are made and kept. Whenever someone else's differences are intolerable to us, they can easily be made the ego's enemy. We see this in our society through the multitude of prejudices people have about each other – a list which seems to be growing.

> *"The body could not separate your mind from your brother's unless you wanted it to be a cause of separation and of distance seen between you and him. Thus, do you endow it (the body) with a power that lies not within itself. And herein lies its power over you."*
> ~ T.29.I.5:1-3

To think that we are somehow different from each other at a fundamental level is insanity. At the bodily level, we all need air to breathe, water to drink, and food to eat. Sadness, anger, and happiness are experienced the same by all of us. Fear, depression, and anxiety grip our minds the same way. Fundamentally, there is no difference between us. We are all more than these bodies – we are formless Mind/Spirit.

> *"The ego always seeks to divide and separate. The Holy Spirit seeks to unify and heal."* ~ T.7.IV.5:2-3

"LAW" OF CHAOS #2:
Each One Must Sin, and
Therefore Deserves Attack and Death

In this second "law" of chaos we see the cycle of insanity perpetuated by condemnation and punishment. We see it operating in the common belief that conflict is the answer to conflict. Whether we are faced with a screaming toddler or a menacing terrorist, we tend to believe that a loud and aggressive response is the ideal answer. Although it may be briefly effective in some cases, it only fuels the ego in the mind of all parties.

What is also notable about this second delusion of the ego

is that it brings to your mind the idea of sin. One of the more radical teachings in the Course is that there is no sin, only mistakes. Sin is an idea of the ego which keeps you locked in its thought system of guilt and fear, so that mistakes cannot possibly be corrected. If you're wondering how one could say a murderer simply made a mistake, I will be explaining in the following chapter on the Right Mind how all of us can be released from the heavy shackles of the idea of sin.

Sin is a product of the thought system of separation. As you have learned, the idea of separation carries with it an immense amount of guilt and also fear. Sinful acts are a result of feeling separate, guilty, and terrified. People "sin" because they are suffering and believe that some sort of attack will help to alleviate their mental anguish, if only for a moment. Believing in sin means believing in punishment; there's no relief for your mind as there's no room for correction or healing to enter.

When we label someone as sinful, we are actually judging them from the perspective of our own guilt. We feel validated in judging others this way and even get a brief sense of relief when we do so. We then demand that they be punished in some manner, another decision driven by the guilt in our minds. This cycle preserves the idea of guilt and only compounds your own suffering.

> *"One way the ego mechanism handles guilt is by projection, so that one's motives and emotions are disowned and seen as being 'out there' and therefore an object for justified hate and vindictiveness."*
> ~ David R. Hawkins, *Transcending the Levels of Consciousness*

Another aspect of the second "law" of chaos is that through our belief in it, we are hindering our salvation from the ego mind. Our connection to Source is vital to healing our mistaken ego identity. Through this second ego delusion, we are telling ourselves that God can't do anything to save us from our sinful ways. If we believe that punishment and attack are the correct responses to error, then we are saying that our individual ego-based will is stronger than God's Will. In our deluded minds, this puts God in a position where It cannot overlook our errors and therefore sin must be real. If God can't save us from our "sins" then how can God save us from the ego? This places us in the position of being unable to ask for and receive the help we need to undo the ego in our minds and heal.

"Its (psychotherapy's) whole function, in the end, is to help the patient deal with one fundamental error; the belief that anger brings him something he really wants, and that by justifying attack he is protecting himself."
~ ACIM: The Process of Psychotherapy:
Introduction.1:5

To stop yourself from giving into this second delusion of the ego, you can become more aware of your judgments of others, and how you react when you're feeling stressed or upset. Healing from the ego mind requires taking responsibility for your beliefs, your actions and reactions. Liberating yourself from the expectations you have for others and the world in general can free your mind from the burden of ideas like sin, attack, and punishment. This is how to feel more relaxed and less reactionary, by letting go of the ideas which make you and others seem guilty.

"Anger always involves projection of separation,

which must ultimately be accepted as one's own re-
sponsibility, rather than being blamed on others."
~ T.6.Introduction:2

"LAW" OF CHAOS #3:
God Believes His Son's Egoic Interpretation of Him and Now Hates His Son

"For if God cannot be mistaken, He must accept His
Son's belief in what he is, and hate him for it." ~ T.23.
II.6:6

Through the third "law" of chaos, our misunderstanding of
our Source leaps farther into madness. Through this ego delusion, we believe that God actually hates and seeks to punish us.
This fear stems from our belief that God is going to punish us
for supposedly walking away from our Source. When we factor
in this third ego delusion, we add God hating us to the mix.

Whenever you feel the sharp pang of fear and begin to
tremble, know that it is your fear of God coming to the surface. Sometimes we can be surprised by what other people are
frightened by; it's easy to see others' fear as an exaggerated
response. Yet when we are not seeing things peacefully ourselves, we try desperately to quiet fearful imaginings, avoid
fearful triggers, or numb the sensation of fear when it creeps
up. No matter what the triggers, we are all afraid because we
believe we are guilty and will face the wrath of God.

"No one who hates but is afraid of love, and therefore
must be afraid of God. He knows not what love means,
he fears to love and loves to hate, and so he thinks that
love is fearful, hate is love." ~ T.29.I.2:3-5

As the above quote suggests, we have inverted the truth so that now love is hate and hate is love. This is a concept so deeply engrained in our world that those who believe that love can heal are often dismissed with a scoff. This is a lot more dangerous than you may think because we are giving ourselves permission to ignore love, which means ignoring what we truly are. It is this third "law" of chaos that preserves the loss of our True Identity. Feelings of loss, depression and loneliness are sure to follow this disconnect from our Source.

> *"And now is conflict made inevitable, beyond the help of God. For now salvation must remain impossible, because the Savior has become the enemy."* ~ T.23. II.7:5-6

Thinking we have been forsaken by our Source is an idea which can only be contrived by the ego. The ego wants to make both God and Love unreliable in our minds. What we need to remember is that God does not know of this world; it is not of Its doing, it is of our doing. And due to the Law of Free Will, which I will be elaborating upon later, God cannot interfere with our wishes; if you want it, so it will be. This terrifies us, so we hide and play victims of a vengeful God.

"LAW" OF CHAOS #4:
You Have What You Have You Taken

> *"By this, another's loss becomes your gain, and thus it fails to recognize that you can never take away save from yourself."* ~ T.23.II.9:4

The final "law" of chaos states that when you take something from another, you remain unaffected by that deed. This delusion follows the ego's law that you give in order to get. It suggests you are safe in doing harm to others and so it is comfortable to see someone as your enemy. Through this insane perception we can become quite fixated on our dislike of others, and our fear that they may take from us or hurt us. This leads us to believe that it's a world of 'eat or be eaten', justifying our attack on others.

"But in a savage world the kind cannot survive, so they must take or else be taken from." ~ T.23.II.10:4

The final "law" of chaos also holds that others must have the missing something which makes you feel complete. This falls in line with the ego's motto that we shall "seek and not find." So we mistakenly look in others for what is truly in ourselves, paradoxically making us suspicious of others. In our daily world we see this dynamic play out as competition, rivalry, and the desire to one-up others. Indulging in these activities becomes our prime motivator for communicating, not to mention the reason why we enter into special love and special hate relationships. The ego needs negativity for fuel. Our relationships thus become battlegrounds and we feel as though we are always at war.

"Therefore, release from guilt requires surrender of this basic egotism because the ego reenergizes itself through the negativity." ~ Dr. David R. Hawkins, *Transcending the Levels of Consciousness*

The Final Principle

The grand finale of the "Laws" of Chaos is the ego's insistence that there is a substitute for love. This insane belief arises in our minds because we have so far been unsuccessful in finding the key to feeling whole. Our idea of love has seemed to let us down and now we feel lost. Believing that we are totally disconnected from peace and the True Love of Source, we imagine there must be something greater than love that can make us feel complete. Simply, we are confused and unsure of what we are really looking for. All we can do is guess that perhaps others hold the key to our salvation. They must have the something which feels missing in our lives. They must be hiding it from us. And *they* believe we are hiding it from *them*.

We also put this uncertainty onto God, unconsciously believing that It must be hiding the substitute for love from us as well. All insane ideas we have about others can easily be transferred to our Source, and this is yet another reason why you may not like the idea of God. This is all a gross misunderstanding; there is no substitute for love. The sense of emptiness we feel is because of the disconnect we presently believe is between us and our Loving Source. No one is hiding the "missing piece" which will make us feel whole again. We are still whole, and already complete. Our True Identity is just clouded over by our belief in these "laws" of chaos.

"These are the laws on which your 'sanity' appears to rest. These are the principles which make the ground beneath your feet seem solid. And it is here you look for meaning. These are the laws you made for your salvation. They hold in place the substitute for Heaven which you prefer. This is their purpose; they were made for this. There is no point in asking what they mean. That is apparent. The means of madness must be insane. Are you as certain that you real-

ize the goal is madness?

No one wants madness, nor does anyone cling to his madness if he sees that this is what it is. What protects madness is the belief that it is true. It is the function of insanity to take the place of truth. It must be seen as truth to be believed. And if it is the truth, then must its opposite, which was the truth before, be madness now. Such a reversal, completely turned around, with madness sanity, illusions true, attack a kindness, hatred love, and murder benediction, is the goal the laws of chaos serve." ~ T.23.II.13:4-13, 14:1-3

For clarity purposes, here is a quick recap of the four "laws" of chaos and the ego's final principle and how they influence your thinking:

"LAW" OF CHAOS #1: *The Truth is Different for Everyone* – Through comparison, the ego highlights the differences in preferences, looks and beliefs between us which the ego uses those differences to initiate and maintain conflict in your mind. Also, this delusion reinforces the ego's idea that we are all indeed separate.

"LAW" OF CHAOS #2: *Each One Must Sin, and Therefore Deserves Attack and Death* – Guilt is strengthened and perpetuated in your mind as sin, punishment and condemnation stem from guilt. The idea of sin comes into play where you believe that you and others are sinful, reinforcing the message that you are guilty and therefore the separation from your Source must be real. Also, your belief in this "law" states that God is unable to save you from your sin making the idea of sin true and making the ego's will of guilt stronger than God's loving Will. And because you believe sin is real, this must mean that God can't save you from your sinful ways which prevents you from accepting the means to your salvation — your oneness with your Source.

"LAW" OF CHAOS #3: *God Believes His Son's Egoic Interpretation of Him and Now Hates His Son* — This delusion cements God as an enemy in your mind for you insanely believe that God agrees that you walked away from It and now hates you for supposedly doing so. This delusion further cements the idea that God is no longer your savior and you are stuck in your guilt and the consequential pain.

"LAW" OF CHAOS #4: *You Have What You Have Taken* — You are somehow able to take from others and remain unaffected by your ego-based thoughts and actions. This sets you up to feel you are safe to have an enemy and judge, condemn, and punish others without harming your own state of mind.

THE FINAL PRINCIPLE: *There is a Substitute for Love* — As you have been unable to find a sense of wholeness and peace in the special love and special hate relationships of the ego's world, you then believe that there must be a substitute for love. This leaves you searching aimlessly in the world for the answer to heal your loneliness. Not being able to find it you grow suspicious of others as you feel they are keeping the answer from you out of vengeance. This keeps you distrustful of others. This suspicion also transfers to God and your Source remains your fearful enemy ready to destroy you.

Each "law" of chaos influences your thinking and tend to be quite subtle. Now that you are aware of them, I encourage you to recall the ego's agenda and its "laws" of chaos whenever you feel upset. Remembering what the ego is trying to accomplish will help you to create some space between ego thoughts and your decision about accepting them as real. Disconnecting from the ego's agenda is something which has been achieved by the enlightened ones who came before us and we are perfectly capable of doing it as well. If you ever feel discouraged and wonder if inner peace is possible for you, remember this teaching from the Course:

> *No one in this world escapes fear, but everyone can reconsider its causes and learn to evaluate them correctly."* ~ ACIM: The Purpose of Psychotherapy – 1:3

As I have shared, our experience with the ego mind is like that of a dream state. Being oblivious to how the ego mind functions keeps your eyes closed to the Truth so that a part of your mind remains asleep, caught in a nightmare. The dream is only desirable if you believe the dream world gives you something of value. In the ego's view, value is a high level of stature, glory or one-upmanship, where for a while you can seem to be above others in intellect, physical appearance, morals, talent, wealth, and so on. The ego also plays the other side of the coin, so value may be placed in a victim-identity: feeling misunderstood, picked upon, or forgotten. Such are the ideas the ego values because they achieve its primary goal: keeping a part of your mind trapped in a dream where your Source and all those around are your enemy, and there is no way out.

"This was the ego – all the cruel hate, the need for ven-

geance and the cries of pain, the fear of dying and the urge to kill, the brotherless illusion and the self that seemed alone in all the universe." ~ Manual for Teachers, Clarification of Terms

CHAPTER TWO

The Right Mind

"The term 'Right-Mindedness' is properly used as the
correction for 'wrong-mindedness,' and applies to the state
of mind that induces accurate perception. It is a miracle
because it heals misperception, and this is indeed a miracle
in view of how you perceive yourself." ~ T.3.IV.4:3-4

"I'm surprised you're not depressed."

THIS is what my mother said to me at the beginning of 2021 when we had finished reviewing all that had happened during my thirties. At the age of thirty-nine, I was happy to see I was coming out of a cycle of intense trial. Between the ages of thirty and thirty-six, I had experienced the worst of a debilitating vertigo disease called Meniere's disease which, along with episodes of extreme vertigo lasting hours, causes deafness and a general dizziness throughout the day. On the heels of Meniere's came a diagnosis of Caregiver's Post Traumatic Stress Disorder, developed from taking care of my dog Guinness while he was sick with cancer. Both challenges offered great opportunities to undo the ego in my mind.

For those who aren't familiar with Meniere's disease, it is known as one of the most psychologically debilitating diseases. For me it induced Visual Dependence, where eyesight compensates for a compromised vestibular system. One comes to rely too much on their vision to get the sense that they are balanced; the result is that if you watch ocean waves coming in and out, or watch snowflakes fall from the sky, you feel that you are also moving with the waves and snowflakes. Looking at anything which is bright or has a strong visual pattern becomes challenging; even combing the lines of products on shelves at a grocery store can throw your balance off.

Bit by bit, a person with Visual Dependence feels increasingly overwhelmed by their environment, inclined to stay at home in order to avoid any discomfort. My world seemed to shrink; I could not enter a grocery store or shopping mall without feeling unbalanced, overwhelmed and anxious. My husband had to do all of our grocery shopping and the simple joy of spending the day clothes-shopping with my mom and sisters was on hold.

Then came the PTSD. Each evening for six weeks before my dog Guinness died, I was repeatedly startled awake by any noise he would make, worried that something horrific was happening. I was on high alert. By the time he passed, my nervous system was shot. Terrible nightmares, sleep paralysis and panic attacks became my norm for the next eleven months until I was finally diagnosed with PTSD and began the journey of calming my nervous system down again.

As this was all happening, I had a brother who was facing a mental health crisis involving alcoholism, suicide attempts, and emotional abuse towards us, his family. In addition, my two beloved in-laws were progressing quickly with Alzheimer's disease and needed more support from my husband Eric and myself. For three years, the mental, physical and emotional demands of each day were at an extreme high.

Thankfully, before this trying time kicked in, I had been a student of the Course for over a decade. I had also been using the Course's advanced form of forgiveness with a genuine commitment since the summer of 2013. I was grateful that I had already created the habit of applying True Forgiveness to any upset I experienced.

Due to my work with the Course, I was keen to the ego's game and was committed to letting Spirit guide me through it all. I knew I wasn't alone and never would be. Because of this, I felt extremely confident that not only would I heal, but that I had the choice to do it with peace and even laughter. This doesn't mean I didn't cry or feel anxious and angry, I certainly did. PTSD is accompanied with some pretty intense anger when you feel your personal boundaries have been crossed. I was particularly surprised by the frequency of dreams in which I was threatening to beat up ghosts who dared to disrupt my peace. The healing path is not always pretty, but you have to look at the ego to let it go. And that's your power: choosing which mind to use as you sort through your issues.

I took great care not to perpetuate all the intense feelings that were boiling up within me by projecting them out onto others or the world in general. Allowing yourself to feel your feelings without ego judgement is what I call 'feeling your feelings safely' – a process which involves observing your feelings with Spirit, ensuring safe passage for them to move through you without making things worse. I was also careful not to label myself as a victim of the disease, PTSD, or any other challenging circumstances.

The Course reframes our trials into opportunities to heal

from the ego thought system. Every time you feel an ego re-action creep up, you can back away peacefully and allow your Higher Self to correct your mistaken ego thinking. That is the essence of Right-Mindedness. Every time I applied Right-Mindedness to an ego reaction, I knew that I was shedding a layer of the ego in my unconscious mind. Implementing Right-Mindedness to our ego-based reactions is *how* the ego is undone in our minds, helping us to be more peaceful and less reactive.

Healing is an attitude. It's a state of mind where you believe that healing is not only possible, but natural. We can also call this being "miracle-minded." Healing can be tricky at times as the ego scrambles to maintain its defenses and keep your loyalty. So, undoing the ego mind does require a firm commit-ment. The fact of the matter is that you're going to look at the ego content in your mind anyway, so why not do it with peace and even a gentle humour?

To help myself through PTSD, I was sure to have more quiet time with Eric and watch more comedies, and I also en-joyed doing Tai Chi in a forest near our home. And of course, I connected with my Source more frequently. These pleasures helped give me a sense that I was on the sane path simply be-cause I felt better and calmer.

We all get to the point where functioning in full ego-mode just isn't possible. Thinking with the ego is a cyclical process of regurgitating ego content and reacting to it as if it were real (projection and perception). Thinking with your Right Mind enables you to hop out of the ego's cycle and move onward with a future free of your past ego attachments. In the Course, we're frequently nudged to give Right-Mindedness a try with the proposition: *"Why delay your happiness?"* A teaching I love! All through the Course there are suggestions reminding us that we suffer needlessly. You have learned a lot about the ego and therefore know *why* it would be best to stop thinking with the ego mind. In this chapter on Right-Mindedness, you will learn more about *how* your mind is healed and Who walks with you on your healing path.

The Right Mind

"...Right-Mindedness is healing." ~ T.2.V.4:5

The Right Mind may be the part of yourself you're mostly unfamiliar with, if you're used to believing in what the ego has to say. But that can change. Your Right Mind can become the only mind you use in this physical experience - that's a choice. As strong as the ego's voice may be right now, there is no doubt you've tuned in to your Right Mind many times throughout your physical experience, as the light of Spirit has always been within your mind. Right-Minded thoughts are more commonly known as inspiration (in-spirit), and they do make their way into your awareness at times, which is a blessing.

In the Course, we are frequently guided to quiet our minds and remember the Truth of Who we are. To be able to remember something means that you knew of it before, but forgot. We are reminded in the Course that just because something is forgotten doesn't mean it's gone. You can think of your Right Mind as the part of your mind which is not only a welcome discovery, but also a reminder of the You that you've forgotten.

This loving part of yourself is what will get you through the sludge of the ego. In the Course we are taught that miracles are natural, which means that it is natural for you to welcome the miracle by switching from your ego mind to your Right

Mind, allowing Spirit to take care of the rest. The key is to stay aligned with Spirit and keep your ego agenda out of the way. This is a practice in itself as we tend to think we know how to do things and what the solutions to our issues should look like. A big part of using your Right Mind is knowing when to back off and let Spirit flow.

Albert Einstein suggested that a problem cannot be solved from the same state of mind which made the problem. The ego mind makes all problems, which keeps you focused on it and thus guarantees its survival. So if the ego mind makes your problems, how can you expect to find solutions there? The ego can only offer truces or remedies which offer you brief relief. Never doubt the ego's reliance on conflict for its survival. All things it offers you, including its "solutions," only hide the one cause of your issues: your belief in separation from your Source. In order to calm the chaos in your life and be open to solutions, you simply must shift out of the ego state. This is known in the Course as being 'above the battleground.' From this higher awareness you access the wisdom of Spirit which guides you directly to peace. All of your solutions will be found through your Right Mind.

It's important to note that the Right Mind is still part of the split mind experience because it is not the One Mind of Spirit. It is the part of your mind which is aware of both the problem and the solution. Whereas the ego mind only knows of the problem, separation, while misidentifying it as a thousand other things. One Mind knows only the Truth of Oneness. Your Right Mind will lead you to your One Mind; it is your way out of hell.

"In order to see, you must recognize that light is within, not without. You do not see outside yourself, nor is the equipment for seeing outside of you. An essential part of this equipment is the light that makes seeing possible. It is with you always, making vision possible in every circumstance." ~ Lesson 44 – 2:1-4

The Voice for the Right Mind

For eons, you have heard and listened to the ego's voice. It is the voice you made the moment you believed in the initial separation idea. Yet, there is another Voice that has always been with you, the Voice which represents Source's Love for you. In the Course, this loving Voice is referred to as the Holy Spirit. I understand that the term Holy Spirit may trigger some people as old Christian definitions get in the way, so I encourage you to find another term which works for you. Many call It Presence and some think of It as the Universe. It manifests in many ways and because It is in everyone's mind, It can communicate or show up in a way which resonates for each individual no matter which faith they believe in, or even if one has no faith. In short, the Holy Spirit is the antidote to the ego mind.

"Right-Mindedness is not to be confused with the knowing mind, because it is applicable only to right perception." ~ T.3.IV.4:1

The Holy Spirit is aware of One Mind and also the split-mind experience. The One Mind is the realm of Knowledge; the split-mind experience of ego consciousness and the Right Mind are both in the realm of perception. Within the split-mind experience, the mind must perceive because it is apart from Knowledge. The Holy Spirit can help you perceive this world correctly, as a realm where people and events are seen without the ego's agenda of conflict. In the Course, we are taught that only perception can be wrong and this is why you must work at the level of the mind to correct your errors. In order to heal your mind, you must heal your perception. I will be sharing more about perception in a later chapter.

"The Holy Spirit is actually your own Higher Self."
~ from *Your Immortal Reality* by Gary R. Renard

I love this quote; it really gave me what I felt was missing from the Catholic teachings I was presented with as a child. Where I was taught that I always needed a liaison, specifically a male priest, to connect with the Holy Spirit for me, *A Course in Miracles* states that the Holy Spirit is literally within me. The Holy Spirit, your loving remedy to all that ails your mind, has always been within you. This is incredibly empowering. Think of all the times you desperately cried out to the heavens for help, when all you really needed was to take some deep breaths, calm your mind and turn inward for the guidance you sought. This is yet another major reason why your mind is so important as it's your access point to the Holy Spirit.

The Holy Spirit's Role

"The Holy Spirit plays an active role in influencing people to go to certain places, meet particular people, and learn the things that will help them the most along the path. It's like the Holy Spirit is nudging you in the right direction." ~ Gary R. Renard, *The Lifetimes When Jesus and Buddha Knew Each Other*

In this experience of separation, you are always choosing between the voice of insanity and the Voice of sanity. For this reason alone, you can see why you would want to choose to listen to your Higher Self – it's perfectly sane and a nice change from the ego's madness. The Holy Spirit knows you are caught in a dream of pain and does not punish you for it. But you punish yourself by remaining within the ego's thought system.

Being 'above the battleground' the Holy Spirit sees the solution possible in every circumstance. Specifically, the Holy Spirit is outside of the realm of linear time and sees all things, past, present and to come, all at once. It is aware of God and also of your ego experience and this is why It is in the prime position to be helpful. It knows our Truth and helps us release our illusions. Through our ego minds, we have only a small, illusory scope in any situation, based upon our very limited individual experiences.

"Thoughts are not big or little: powerful or weak. They are merely true or false." ~ Lesson 16

The Holy Spirit uses what is known as True Perception: a way of perceiving this world without latching onto it. Through True Perception, things are seen as either true or false. Perceiving with the ego is called misperception as it leads to a misunderstanding of objects, people and circumstances because everything is incorrectly endowed with the ego's agenda of chaos. Because the ego itself is nothing, any time you perceive with it you are investing in what is false. According to your Higher Self, only that which is love and leads to peace is true. The Holy Spirit's True Perception is very clear and is not subject to degrees or levels. In this regard, it is the simplicity you need to cut through the absurd complexity of the ego's thought system.

"The only safety lies in extending the Holy Spirit, because as you see His gentleness in others your own mind perceives itself as totally harmless." ~ T.6.III.3:1

Specifically, the Holy Spirit's role is to free your mind of attack and fear thoughts. Your perception is polluted by fear, leading you to regard others and this world with anxiety. With the ego, you use your own mind as a weapon against yourself. Yet the Holy Spirit guides you to correct your thinking, leading to the healing of your mind. As attack thoughts dissolve you begin to see yourself, others, and the world peacefully. The result is that you perceive your own mind as harmless and that is the essence of true inner peace.

The Holy Spirit's True Perception turns the ego's world upside down. What the ego promotes as necessary fear, anger, sadness and anxiety, the Holy Spirit reframes as calls for love. To the Holy Spirit, the only answer to anything is love, for to do anything else would perpetuate the ego's insane thought system. While the ego would say you are validated by being a victim, the Holy Spirit puts you in the seat of power, reminding you that you made this world. It also invites you to remember that you are fully able to choose *how* you want to perceive your world and the people who seemed to wrong you.

Here are a few miracle principles which share how the mind is truly healed of its mistaken thinking:

- Miracle Principle 17 – *"Miracles transcend the body. They are sudden shifts into invisibility, away from the bodily level. That is why they heal."*

- Miracle Principle 32 - *"I (Jesus as One with the Holy Spirit) inspire all miracles, which are really intercessions. They intercede for your holiness and make your perceptions holy. By placing you beyond the physical laws they raise you into the sphere of the celestial order. In this order you are perfect."*
- Miracle Principle 33 – *"Miracles honour you because you are lovable. They dispel illusions about yourself and perceive the light in you. They thus atone for your errors by freeing you from your nightmares. By releasing your mind from the imprisonment of your illusions, they restore your sanity."*
- Miracle Principle 36 – *"Miracles are examples of right thinking, aligning your perceptions with truth as God created it."*

When we ask our Higher Self for help, we are asking to forget the ego and not use its feelings for validation. This is a necessary change in our thinking. The mind always needs a focus, so as you let your old ego perceptions go, your mind can rightfully focus on Spirit. In lesson 313 of the Course, we are guided to claim a new way of perceiving this world by saying; *"Now let a new perception come to me."* As your mind focuses on Spirit, your thinking will align with the Truth. Experiencing True Perception is not really difficult; the only challenge is the willingness to be wrong about the judgements you've made about yourself and others. This willingness allows a far more peaceful perception to arise in your mind.

The Classroom

"Can you imagine what it means to have no cares, no worries, no anxieties, but merely to be perfectly calm and quiet all the time? Yet, that is what time is for; to learn just that and nothing more." ~ T.15.1.1:1-2

My father sat before me, dismayed, angry, and almost defeated. My three-year-old nephew, Jude, had just been diagnosed with leukemia and today he was being admitted to the hospital to begin extensive treatment. After shedding some tears and discussing how we could be of best help to my sister and my brother-in-law, my Dad and I sat and had a conversation about the purpose of life in general.

"Why?" my father muttered. "Why do we bother saving money? We work and we save money to be settled one day... you hope. But you don't settle, there's always fucking something. Always."

I understood my Dad's frustration. He had retired a few months earlier and was looking to settle into a new phase of relaxation, finally getting "some head peace," in Northern Irish lingo. Now, the notion of true peace hung delicately like a feather before my father's face, ready to disappear at the slightest sigh. My father has been in search of peace his whole life and he'd recently hoped that retirement would be the key to feeling it. But with one diagnosis another chance at peace was gone.

Or was it?

Our sweet Jude has recovered but it was a major lesson for us all as a family. The questions of *"What is really important?"*

and *"Why are we really here?"* naturally come to one's mind when faced with something so threatening as the sickness and potential demise of a child. The tragic circumstances which occur in our world can be not only frightening, but seem utterly purposeless. That's how the ego would always have it.

I was not willing to hear what the ego had to say about Jude. As a student of the Course, I knew this trial held the purpose of healing and by God, I was not going to waste this powerful lesson! If I went the ego's route, I would miss the lesson completely. If I took the Holy Spirit's hand, I was going to heal and my beautiful nephew would be one of my many teachers in this life.

"When you wake in the morning realize that you are in a class to unlearn what your ego taught you." ~ Kenneth Wapnick, *Ending Our Resistance to Love*, pg. 36

I have always appreciated the Course's teaching that this world is a classroom; it takes the edge off when you feel like you've done something wrong. This world isn't perfect and it's never going to be perfect. It is a product of the ego mind. Within this classroom, you're not always going to get things perfectly right and that's fine. You're also not going to be exempt from class and skip class on your ego, yet that's fine as well. Experiencing is *how* you learn. Intellectually you can know things, but the mind learns best through experience.

The physical world is where that ego content plays out, and you experience the results of your decisions to think with either the ego or your Higher Self. You learn by the feelings that result from how you think. This is known as cause and effect, which I will share more about in an upcoming chapter. When you feel out of accord with peace, in any way, that's your red flag that you've chosen the ego. Seeing beyond the ego's façade to the Truth is at the core of each lesson you encounter. That is where the Holy Spirit comes in. H.S. will help you look at your ego safely. To the ego, this world is where you hide from God; to the Holy Spirit, this world is where you learn.

Specifically, this world serves no other purpose than to teach us the ego isn't real and God is. As we invite the Holy Spirit's True Perception, the classroom will transform into the Real World, correctly perceived with the Holy Spirit. In the Real World experience, you are detached from the ego's agenda and see all things as reflections of love. By clearing your mind of ego, which can only be done in physical experience, you are prepping your mind to accept the ineffable love of God. With the amount of conflict you carry in your mind at present, you may not feel worthy of God's love. Your unfounded guilt remains a heavy burden and prevents you from accepting love in worldly relationships, much less the unconditional love of God.

The classroom is an essential step in your enlightenment and for this reason it holds great purpose. The trials of this world are not meant to knock you back. With the Holy Spirit's help, they are intended to lift you above the chaos. In this regard, your trials are deeply meaningful. Even the most trivial trial like a disagreement with your partner is a gateway to your awareness of God's love. As mundane as some of your trials may seem, they still block your mind's full awareness of Source and you do need to look at them. The same goes for the seemingly bigger trials which come up. Again, they need to be looked at so they can be healed. Your trials are your stepping stones to God.

It's important to remember that our classroom trials do not come from the spiritual realm, they come from the ego content of our unconscious minds. The Holy Spirit's role is to look at the trials with us so they are perceived correctly and the mind is healed. This requires a total reversal in how you think presently, but it's the only way out of the ego's thought system. When a trial pops up, you can see it as the Holy Spirit giving you a vote of confidence that you are ready and able to look at your fears safely.

In the Course, we are taught that our life's script is written. This means that all our trials were determined by us before we appeared to enter these bodies. My experience with Meniere's disease and PTSD is part of my life's script. Jude getting leukemia was part of his. Your experiences are part of yours. It's senseless then to lament our trials. It makes far more sense to use them to wake up as they hold no other purpose. Try not to be tempted to use them to deceive yourself.

"It takes great learning to understand that all things, events, encounters, and circumstances are helpful." ~ Manual for Teachers.4.I.A4:5

What you have chosen to experience stems from the unconscious, but you can consciously choose *how* to respond to these experiences: with either ego or Spirit. That is your true power in this world. The ego would have you think all experriences came from outside yourself, which only preserves the insane idea that you are a powerless victim. As unsettling and traumatic some of our trials may be, they are going to be either prolonged or healed by choice of which mind to perceive them with.

As your mind heals, time itself dissolves. This is one of the more radical teachings in the Course: time disappears once it has served its purpose of allowing a lesson to occur. Consciously, we experience time in a linear fashion, which Kenneth Wapnick compared to a red carpet rolling out. As you learn a lesson, there is no need for you to play out the lesson again in the future so a section of red carpet which would present yet another opportunity for you to learn your lesson disappears.

It is helpful to have a grasp on the fact that this physical world and all its seeming fundamentals, like time, are illusory. We can use them for the purposes of healing, and when that great need is met, they simply disappear from our mind's awareness. More insights can be found in Kenneth Wapnick's book *A Vast Illusion: Time According to A Course in Miracles.*

> *"Each day should be devoted to miracles. The purpose of time is to enable you to learn how to use time constructively. It is thus a teaching device and a means to an end. Time will cease when it is no longer useful in facilitating learning."* ~ T.1.I.15

A Mistake to be Corrected

Earlier I mentioned how our belief in sin keeps us stuck in a cycle of guilt, condemnation and fear. Sin says you did something wrong. The Holy Spirit has a different opinion: you couldn't have done anything wrong, thus you are innocent. The Holy Spirit's perception is based on the fact that the separation never occurred and that you're having a dream. If you never actually walked away from your Source then there is nothing to feel guilty about. From this fresh perspective the "sins" of this world are seen by the Holy Spirit as mistakes. Sins are punished and keep you locked in the thought system of guilt and fear, whereas mistakes can be corrected and lead to healing. Healing is natural according to the Course, meaning that you can always step out of the cycle of guilt.

Mistaken thinking stems from the initial wrong belief that you are the ego. Once you have decided that you are a separate ego, your thinking will naturally follow your chosen trajectory: *"Every system of thought must have a starting point. It begins with either a making (ego) or a creating (Spirit)..."* ~ T.3.VII.1:1-2. Remember that you believe you are the ego, and thus you take its dictates seriously. You think that you are listening to your true self, and this way of thinking will reinforce separation until you actively choose to think differently. It is fortunate for us all that we are able to change our minds.

Scientists now accept the idea that the brain has a plastic nature, meaning it can still change neurologically when fully developed. The brain is an effect of the mind and its plasticity is due to the mind's malleability. Old habits of mistaken thinking can be overridden with new and healthy Right-Minded habits, which means that you are *never* stuck in your way of thinking. Our salvation from the ego mind relies upon our minds ability to think differently. Our belief that we are guilty and sinful *can* change.

Seeing the "sins" of yourself and others as mistakes requires a major change in perception. We are so used to judging everyone through sinful eyes that to see a "sin" as a mistake may feel like you're letting someone else off the hook too easily. "Sinful" people can be vicious, so the ego mind will question why you want to see them compassionately. It's therefore helpful to remember why the ego wants condemnation, punishment, and retaliation – all this keeps the ego going and imprisons your mind. This is why you feel obligated to maintain guilt and fear. Yet, as we're lovingly reminded in the Course, this need not be.

From an ACIM perspective, only someone who is suffering could attack another. There must be some sort of mental angst which causes them to project. When you recognize this, it's easier to change your perception from seeing someone as "sinful" to calling for love. Through this Right-Minded perception, our minds are relieved of the heaviness of a perception of guilt. The Holy Spirit would take this one step further and remind you that what you see in the world is a projection of the ego mind. The ego mind appears to be split into billions of individual minds and your power seems limited to the part you are experiencing. Even though billions of people may feed into the idea of guilt, your power is to step out of ego-mode, recognize that what you are seeing is a projection, and that you have the ability to change your mind about what you are seeing.

Through your Right Mind, your enemy becomes someone who needs a reminder of peace and not a reinforcement of the insanity of guilt. Someone who is suffering does not need their guilt compounded, as that leads only to more guilt and its tragic consequences. If you really want to free your mind, it is essential that you practice reframing your ideas of guilt in a Right-Minded way. For example, when I think of someone who has committed murder, my hope for them is that they get the mental rehabilitation and education they require while they are incarcerated. Through doing so, their minds can heal and a portion of the ego thought system dissolves along with its madness.

I recall an episode of Oprah where a grieving mother was

featured. This mother went to a prison to meet the man who shot and killed her son. Looking for closure, the mother walked away with much more; she developed a loving mother-son relationship with the man who killed her child. The murderer admitted that her act of forgiveness and compassion transformed him. He admitted that when she held his hand and forgave him, that was his first experience of love. This man now had a chance to heal his mind. That's the Holy Spirit at work.

I encourage you to ask yourself: *"How can I expect to have inner peace while I hold onto thoughts of guilt about myself and others?"* How can you expect to remember your Oneness with your Source if you foster guilt and punishment in your mind? Your Source *knows* we are all One, and no one is left out of the state of mind known as heaven. If you judge another as guilty, you have gone in a completely different direction from peace and Oneness. You can get back on the spiritual track though, and the Holy Spirit will support your choice. Seeing others as inherently innocent, like yourself, is a vital step towards inner peace. When anyone acts from ego, recognize it is a mistake worthy only of correction.

Connecting with the Holy Spirit

*"The Holy Spirit speaks to **you**."* ~ T.27.V.1:10

Receiving a message from your Higher Self is an illuminating experience. You may have had a day when everything that happened felt synchronistic. And I'm sure you've had some *"A-ha!"* moments in your life as well. These experiences are a result of the Holy Spirit flowing through your mind. They have a certain feel and quality to them which you can't reproduce on your own. I liken these experiences to the feeling of a perfect summer wind which gently wraps around you and refreshes you. It's exactly what you need and it feels so good.

To connect with the Holy Spirit, all that is required is that you step back from your thoughts about any difficult situation and ask for help. Making that simple request says so much; it declares that you are done with conflict, if even for a moment, and that you're no longer willing to go it alone. Your belief in separation is your core mental issue. When you choose to handle things on your own, you are reinforcing separation and you can be certain you will feel fear, guilt and loneliness as a result. You know what those feel like and you don't need to go back to them.

If you want inner peace, then reaching out for help is exactly what you want to do. You need support in getting out of the ego's thought system, but the support you need does not come from someone or something outside yourself, it comes from within. I encourage you not to get stuck on the idea that there is a "me" and a "Holy Spirit" – that implies separation. Dismiss the idea of a separate "me" and fully accept the idea that you are one with the Holy Spirit. For at no point does separation actually exist.

Turning to the Holy Spirit can be very casual and deeply meaningful at the same time. It's natural to turn to your Higher Self so you don't have to worry about being ritualistic. The Holy Spirit is the chill part of your Mind and knows that you're only going to use It if you feel good about it and not forced into it. Quite simply, if you're feeling forced, you're not in your Right Mind anyway. A wonderful part of Right-Mindedness is that it brings you to your happy place. When it becomes a habit to be happy, you will be quicker to realize when you're upset and want to correct your thinking immediately.

You also want to be alert to the ego's notion that you are unworthy or incapable of connecting with the Holy Spirit. This is a big hurdle for some people to jump over. The guilt in your unconscious mind is the reason you feel unworthy of so many things. Try to remember that this deep sense of unworthiness is how you stay in the ego's thought system, and don't feel motivated to move beyond it. Yet, you are probably aware that you can't stay in the ego's pain forever; it's frankly unsustainable. You don't want this false self running the show as you'll just be running in circles.

Another hiccup in turning to the Holy Spirit may be that you are afraid of losing the world you made. We've been experiencing the ego for seeming eons and as chaotic as it may be, it's still familiar. It's like a bad relationship in which we're "comfortable in conflict." It's strange that the Voice which tells us that we are loving, innocent, and deserving of peace is so foreign to us. This is why it is so helpful to learn what the ego is up to. Once recognized, its thought system is transparent, and its chaos so undesirable, that turning to the Holy Spirit becomes increasingly attractive.

How the Holy Spirit Speaks to You

Being the messenger of peace, you can trust that the Holy Spirit's message will always lead to just that. Earlier I shared that a message from the Holy Spirit feels like the comfort of a summer breeze. For further clarity I can say that a message from the Holy Spirit is accompanied by a sensation of enthusiasm and a recognition that you're on the right path. The feeling is that there is nothing else you'd rather do than what you've been guided to do. As the Holy Spirit is in your mind, it will show up mainly through messages in your mind in any of these forms:

- Stroke of inspiration
- Novel idea
- Intuition
- Messages in dreams
- A song, sign, or message from someone that strikes a chord

Due to the forms in which the Holy Spirit's guidance shows up, it's important to keep your mind open and quiet so that past ego learnings and current expectations do not steal your focus.

"In quietness are all things answered, and is every problem quietly resolved. In conflict there can be no answer and no resolution, for its purpose is to make no resolution possible, and to ensure no answer will be plain." ~ T.27.IV.1:1-2

Allowing the Miracle

A popular Course quote is *"Miracles are natural. When they do not occur, something has gone wrong."* ~ T.1.I.6:1-2 The thing which has gone wrong is that we have not allowed ourselves to receive the miracle.

How many times have you asked for help from Spirit and then felt like you received no answer? As we are so used to thinking with the ego, we tend to think we already know what the answer to our problems should be, when they should be resolved, and how healing should occur. So if Spirit could just listen to us and let that happen, that would be great. Yet when we dictate to Spirit how things should be, we are repeating the tiny, mad idea. We are again saying that we want to be the creator in control.

Asking the Holy Spirit for help is not just an invitation. To actually welcome the miracle requires a letting-go of what past ego-based thoughts have to say about the situation. You're not going to receive the miracle (a correction of your thinking) by using your Right Mind to ask for help and then switching to your ego mind to control the outcome. Remember that the Holy Spirit, your Higher Self, is way above the battleground and sees all things, past, present and to come. It knows what to do. Our limited ego-scope will only bring us more of what we had in the past because that's all it knows. Step out of the way and let yourself receive.

"You can be as vigilant against the ego's dictates as for them." ~ T.4.IV.4:2

As long as you want to stop doing things with the ego and start using your Higher Self, that's a good enough invitation for the Holy Spirit. When faced with an issue, my sisters and I simply remind each other to *"H.S. it"* or *"Lift it upstairs,"* referring to lifting the situation up to the spiritual realm. All miracles occur in the mind and at times you will see physical effects of these miracles. In my experience, some of these effects have taken a few months to show up – and sometimes nothing happens except that I feel peaceful, which is an amazing gift in itself.

"I merely follow for I would not lead." ~ Lesson 324

Asking the Holy Spirit for help is about following, not leading. We don't know how to lead. In Gary Renard's work, we are taught that Jesus wasn't the ultimate leader, he was the ultimate follower. He developed his mind to the point that he only paid attention to the Voice of the Holy Spirit. In so doing, he became enlightened. This is also possible for you. You don't need to go through life thinking you're alone anymore.

A Course in Miracles offers two affirmations you can use to bring the Holy Spirit to the forefront of awareness: First, that upon awakening in the morning, connect with the Holy Spirit and invite Its guidance. Personally, I like to say; *"Today, I will make no decisions by myself. I know You are with me, Holy Spirit. I take Your hand."* This places you in your Right Mind after a night's rest and helps to shake off the ego. You can word your morning greeting to the Holy Spirit in a way that best suits you, just be sure to feel the connection and remember you're not alone.

Also, you can place yourself in the service of the Holy Spirit by repeating this prayer from ACIM:

"I am here only to be truly helpful
I am here to represent Him Who sent me
I do not have to worry about what to say or what to do
Because He Who sent me will direct me
I am content to be wherever He wishes
Knowing He goes there with Me
I will be healed as I let Him teach me to heal"
~ T.2.V-A.18:2-6

The Correction

"Only Right-Mindedness can correct in a way that has any real effect." ~ T.2.V.A.14:2

Using your Right Mind involves implementing the principle known as the Atonement, which reminds us that we never left our Source. The Atonement is the one idea which undoes *all* ego ideas. If it seems simple, that's because it is. Remember that the ego wants to get you caught up in its tangled mess of chaos and complexity. Spirit is very simple because it represents the perfect gleaming Truth that only our Source is real and nothing else is. The essence of the Atonement can be summed up perfectly in the statement, **God is**. Nothing can replace the Will of the Source; you can only dream that there is something different out there.

All Right-Minded principles reflect the Atonement and draw you away from judging this world as if it were real. As I have shared, your mind always needs a focus, so when you are not aware of the ego your mind is free to connect with Spirit. Instead of cementing your attachment to this world, Right-Minded principles allow you to function peacefully within the world as they bring your focus above the chaos.

Right-Minded principles include:

- Non-judgment
- True Forgiveness
- Holy Instant (The Instant you choose the Holy Spirit over the ego)
- True Perception
- True Denial

There is a wonderful Course lesson which I utilize often: *"Truth will correct all errors in my mind."* (#107). As you know, all your issues begin with the ego mind, meaning they begin with thoughts. As the ego is a mistaken thought, all it takes to correct it is a True thought: the Atonement. When you accept one ego thought as true, it's too easy to take all the following ego thoughts seriously. Yet if you stop to correct one ego thought, you change the trajectory of your thinking and stop yourself from spiraling deeper into the ego's thought system. Inner peace begins with such a simple correction.

Application of the Atonement is easy to do and requires nothing more than a quiet moment where you are willing to remember the Truth. When I think about the Atonement I see it as a protection in my mind, something which helps me not feel tempted to delve into the ego's world. The Atonement simply reminds you that what you are seeing in the world is not your Reality. You may be experiencing this world for a time, and it is important to acknowledge that; if you were to deny this world, you would be denying the power of your mind. It's very important that you honor the power of your mind so then you are not tempted to misuse it and diminish its incredible strength. It is possible to accept that a part of your mind is asleep and dreaming while you remember that your True Self is at Home.

Your application of the Atonement is the best way to become lucid in this dream world. As you remind yourself of Where you really are, you react less to this physical world. Then you are better able to perceive this world through the Holy Spirit's True Perception. This is where seeing this world as a dream really comes in handy. You don't deny the dream, you just chalk it up to something you experience with your mind. Don't deny it. Use it as the teaching device it's meant to be.

The Atonement also helps you to make friends with God again. Remember from the "laws" of chaos that we think God is our enemy, and we are terrified God will punish us. A major part of healing your mind requires rekindling your relationship with your Source. This is something I will be sharing about in the next chapter. Application of the Atonement principle reminds you of your Oneness with your Source and allows your mind to back out of the ego's thought system.

"Corrected error is the error's end." ~ T.25.III.4:2

Personally, I have not reached the point where I am in constant perfect communication with the Holy Spirit, but I have committed to strengthening my relationship. Consequently I feel and experience the benefits of doing so every day. My connection to the Holy Spirit is what gave me the confidence to move positively forward through each panic attack when PTSD was at its worst. And when I felt magnetized to the couch or bed in the hours-long sessions of vertigo, the Holy Spirit was there to help me feel safe and just let it pass. It's also what told me that even though I may not be able to comfortably go into a grocery store and feel balanced, I'm still okay and it's really not a big deal.

Most importantly, the strongest message I've received from the Holy Spirit is that when I'm facing a trial, that trial is not forever. With the Holy Spirit, I am reminded that healing is natural and if I forgive right now, I free my future of my past fears and I become more present in the eternal now.

> *"Christ's vision has one law. It does not look upon a body, and mistake it for the Son whom God created. It beholds a light beyond the body; an idea beyond what can be touched, a purity undimmed by errors, pitiful mistakes, and fearful thoughts of guilt from dreams of sin. It sees no separation. And it looks on everyone, on every circumstance, all happenings and all events, without the slightest fading of the light it sees."*
> ~ Lesson 158.7:1-5

CHAPTER THREE

The One Mind

"The innocence of God is the true state of the mind of His Son. In this state your mind knows God, for God is not symbolic; He is fact." ~ T.3.I.8:1-2

IN THE spring of 2016, I healed from the supposedly "incurable" Meniere's disease, thanks to my acknowledgement of my Oneness in Source. I feel that I am meant to share this healing story to anyone who may need to hear it. I reflect upon it when I need a loving reminder of my True Identity.

Healing of your mind is a *result* of Right-Minded thinking. Sometimes physical ailments will also heal. True healing means that you are no longer in fear, so that your mind is no longer accepting the ego's opinion of what you're experiencing. Instead your mind fully accepts your Reality, replacing the ego in your mind. When you accept the Truth then it doesn't really matter what happens to you here in this physical experience, because you know it is a dream. This is an advanced state that you will inevitably reach.

The healing sequence is this: Atonement is the *principle*, the miracle is the *means* and healing is the *result*. When you apply the Atonement to your thinking, healing is the result – this is basic cause and effect. As I stated in the previous chapter,

Atonement is the recognition that we never actually separated from our Source. This one idea is so powerful it completely undoes the entire ego thought system. Try not to be deceived by its simplicity. Remember that the ego is only a mistaken idea. It can only be corrected by a Right-Minded idea, leading your mind to accept that only God is real.

IN MARCH of 2016, after recovering from a six-hour bout of vertigo, my husband and my mother urged me to visit an Ear, Nose and Throat (ENT) specialist to find out why the vertigo was so extreme and prolonged. I asked my doctor for the referral and my ENT specialist appointment was set for two months later. Two months may seem like a long time to wait for an appointment but intuitively I knew I was being given a great opportunity and some time to implement True Forgiveness before the appointment. I had recalled three years earlier reading about Gary Renard's healing experiences from a powerful meditation in his book *Love Has Forgotten No One* (p. 79), and I was excited to give it a try for myself.

For the next two months, I got to work. With each fearful thought and ego reaction to a symptom of Meniere's disease, I applied True Forgiveness. Every evening, I did the healing meditation in Gary's book. After a few weeks, I was delighted to notice that the telltale sensation of Meniere's disease, wherein one's ear feels plugged up with water, had disappeared. For the first time in over a decade, the accompanying sound of "listening to a seashell" was also gone and I could hear clearly out of my right ear. This was an incredible result considering I wasn't really concerned with that particular symptom, but there was still more to come.

Two days before the ENT appointment I simply felt better and wasn't afraid of vertigo recurring. As I have shared, all healing is essentially the release from fear. Due to the peace I was feeling, I felt strongly that I didn't need the appointment. I told my husband, Eric, how I was feeling and he lovingly encouraged me to keep the appointment. Uncertain as to what to do, I decided to go upstairs to our bedroom to connect with H.S. about it all. I calmed my mind and gave the details of the appointment and the idea of vertigo over to the Holy Spirit to handle for me. I stated clearly that I knew no matter what happened with my body, it was all for my forgiveness and to remind me of my True Identity as being innocent and perfectly One with my Source. I refused to accept what the ego had to say, and I was firm that whatever my Higher Self guided me to do, I would happily do. I rested my mind in the Truth.

After connecting with H.S., I began walking down the stairs. As I did, my eyes rested upon a statue of the Buddha we have on our landing. In that moment, it came to me: *"Buddha was a man. Jesus was a man. They became enlightened. If they can do it then so can I!"* A strong energy pulsed through my body and I declared in my mind *"That's it! I am One in God! That's my True Identity and I will accept nothing less!"* I carried on with my day in confidence knowing that I was right to have left my ego out of everything and to trust in Spirit.

The next day, a curious thing happened; the ENT specialist's receptionist called to say that my appointment the next day had to be cancelled. I knew then that my intuition about the appointment had been correct. That evening, I had a vivid dream in which I entered the bathroom and stared into the large bathroom mirror. Then, I felt a tickle in my right ear. I took my right pinky and used my nail to scratch the tickle. I was astonished to see black oil start to pour out of my ear. The oil was splashing all over me, the bathroom and the mirror. Also, to my surprise, a little monkey hand came out of my ear which I immediately attributed to the ego because I jokingly call the ego a "cheeky lil' monkey."

After some time, the oil stopped flowing and I looked into the mirror to see a brighter version of myself. In that moment, I felt a lightness run up the right side of my neck, through my ear and out the top of my head. Then, I woke up. I recalled the dream immediately and knew I had been healed. Five years later, I have not had any problems with vertigo or my hearing. The supposedly "incurable" disease is now gone and it was because I firmly accepted my Oneness with my Source.

A physical effect of the idea of separation, the Meniere's disease, was healed by my mind's acceptance of the only healing idea, the Atonement. I still tear up when I recall this experience. Truly, we are not the ego at all. With absolute confidence I say to you, **you are a fundamental part of God.** You don't need to settle for anything less.

God is pure creative power and you are able to create because of this fact. God's Mind is your Mind. More specifically, you are *in* the Mind of God. Right now, you are misusing this creative power whenever you choose the ego. I shared earlier that your mind is always creating and never sleeps. This is because you are always in the Mind of God even though you're having a dream of something else. Try not to be afraid that your mind is always creating. In this section, you will be reminded of What You really are, which will help you to realize that there really is nothing to fear.

Redefining God

Just as some struggle with the term "Holy Spirit" or the idea of Jesus, there are many who can't get on board with God. Yet even if you love God, there is still a deep part of you which is fearful of your Source. We covered why this is so in the section on the "laws" of chaos – you're afraid that God agrees with your ego's opinion that you are guilty and deserve to be punished. As long as you have guilt in your mind, you will perceive through that guilt, skewing your understanding of everything, including God.

> *"You have been fearful of everyone and everything. You are afraid of God, of me (Jesus) and of yourself. You have misperceived or miscreated Us, and believe in what you have made. You would not have done this if you were not afraid of your own thoughts."*
> ~ T.2.VII.5:6-7

Mistakenly, we believe that all our thoughts and actions are being judged by a condemnatory god. Every time something goes awry in our world, we mistakenly think it's because we are being punished by this angry god. It's hard to relax when you feel that you are constantly under an all-powerful surveillance. Every twinge of guilt suggests that we've buggered up somehow and will be horribly punished by our maker. With this grossly skewed perception, it's no wonder why people choose to be atheists or make needless sacrifices to appease the wrath of a vengeful god.

To "protect" ourselves from this god's punishment, we hide behind the body and the physical world. Doing so, we forget that we even have a mind which needs to be acknowledged, respected and nurtured. Instead we focus on bodily needs, getting more entrenched in the world to avoid facing judgement. In this physical experience, where the real God of Love seems absent, the ego uses our bodies and its five senses to certify the "evidence" that this world is real and God isn't. This leads us to another radical teaching of the Course: God isn't actually aware of this world. To do so would mean God could perceive the ego's insanity, but God knows nothing of what we've made. Guilt, disease, and death are unfathomable to the perfection of the One Mind.

> *"Is it not strange that you believe to think you made the world you see is arrogance? God made it not. Of this you can be sure. What can He know of the ephemeral, the sinful and the guilty, the afraid, the suffering and lonely, and the mind that lives within a body that must die? You but accuse Him of insanity, to think He made a world where such things seem to have reality. He is not mad. Yet only madness makes a world like this."* ~ Lesson 152: 6:1-7

To be able to perceive insanity would mean that your Source isn't perfect. If God were to acknowledge this insane world as being real, then the Mind of God would believe insanity and imperfection are real. In truth, God knows nothing of the ego because the ego isn't real. Source also has no need for perception because perception is an attribute of the split mind. As I shared in the previous chapter, the One Mind of Source *knows* what is real and has no questions. In the ego experience, perception takes the place of knowledge. While the One Mind knows, the ego mind questions.

The Holy Spirit is the representative for God in this physical experience. Remember that the Holy Spirit is aware of God and the ego without believing in the ego and its illusions. Although your Source is unaware of this world, It is still aware of the True You. I mentioned earlier that this physical experience is being dreamed by a tiny part of your mind. As I have stated, the majority of your Mind knows where It truly is. In the Course, the split mind is likened to a ripple in the ocean or a ray of sunshine – still one with the ocean, still one with the sun, but having an experience of thinking it is alone. In this physical experience, you are the ripple in the deep ocean, a ray of sunshine which exists only because of the sun. You are one with everything while dreaming you are apart from everything.

As a reminder, the underlying current of fear and distrust in yourself come from these mistaken ideas:

- That you will be punished by God for supposedly separating from It
- That you will choose to separate again and feel the immense discomfort of guilt

The harm of thinking God made this world is that you blame God for the ego's insanity. We ask why God took a child or caused bankruptcy or simply declined to answer a desperate prayer. All the insanity, emptiness, and pain that the world seems to cause us is blamed on God. God is formless, so it's easy to channel our pain and anger toward an entity we cannot see or feel. People also blame the so-called devil for the same atrocities that God supposedly committed. It's comparable to "flaming" someone online; it's easier to attack someone who is far away and invisible to you. You don't have to look anyone in the eye. So, you swear and continue to be afraid of God when all the while it was your investment in the ego which caused your pain.

I have shared that one of our tasks in this physical realm is to rekindle our relationship with God. I frequently encourage others to embrace their Oneness with Source by connecting and being grateful to It. One of the hang-ups I hear about this process is really a statement of disbelief: "Can *I* really connect with God?" Know that connecting with God is easier and more natural to you than breathing. You *are* because God *is*. Never are you apart.

Along with putting the Holy Spirit in charge of my thinking at the beginning of the day, I like to say hello to God and feel Love flow through me. I also enjoy taking moments of connection with Source throughout my day. Sometimes just for a minute and often for ten minutes, I sit down and forgive myself for thinking that I could or would walk away from my true love. Then I express gratitude that the separation never happened and that I'm safe and taken care of in every way. I find my connection sessions very therapeutic and essential to maintaining a calm mind and a Right-Minded perspective.

Throughout the Course lessons, we are frequently encouraged to move past all the thoughts of this world and connect with our Source. This is a practice which is easy for a trained mind and difficult for an untrained mind. Focusing on conflict and chaos is what an untrained mind does. For just a moment, you can lay aside the ego's thoughts of hate and pain and practice making space in your awareness for the memory of God to come forth. In the Course, we are taught that memories do not have to reflect only the past; they can just as easily be a thought of the present moment. Our present moment, unobstructed by the painful memories of the ego, is the ongoing memory of God. This is why the present moment is so powerful: the awareness of God is there.

Redefining You

"A co-creator with the Father must have a Son. Yet must this Son have been created like Himself. A perfect being, all-encompassing and all-encompassed, nothing to add and nothing taken from; not born of size nor place nor time, nor held to limits or uncertainties of any kind." ~ T.24VII.7:1-3

After eons of listening to the ego, we have forgotten not only our Source but Who we truly are. Unconsciously terrified of how powerful our minds are, we have allowed ourselves to be continuously belittled by the ego's opinion of us. We are taught in the Course that our problem of connecting with God is not one of concentration, but low self-evaluation. We do not feel worthy of God's Love and so we quickly discard the idea that we are able to connect with It. Feeling unworthy is the core reason you don't commit to your spiritual practice or any other discipline which will help you calm and train your mind. Your sense of unworthiness is due to the guilt in your mind, which needs to be undone so you can begin to feel you are worthy of your True Identity and the uncompromising love of your Source.

Thankfully, your worth has been determined by your Source and not the ego. You may dream you are something shameful and unlovable, but of course that is not your Reality.

The fact is that you were created by your Source, so Who you truly are is not up for debate. The ego is known as the questioning mind and your identity is an ideal topic for the ego to question. You don't want to turn to something so uncertain and conflicted to tell you about your worth and identity. If you struggle with thinking that you could be more than your body and more than your mistakes, then you can begin by simply opening your mind to the idea that perhaps you have just forgotten yourself.

With each ego thought you take seriously, a 'veil of forgetfulness' clouds your mind. This is how you forgot your True Identity. Therefore, remembering your True Self is a process of undoing the mistaken ego identity which has clouded your awareness. Give yourself the chance to get there. I understand that self-esteem and worthiness are triggering topics for some people but this is not about forcing yourself to accept something you're not ready for; it's about letting yourself remember. As you commit to Right-Mindedness, your awareness of what is real and what isn't will become clearer.

You don't need to fully accept all these ideas right away, you can just be open. When I struggle with accepting that I am One in God or have concern that a Right-Minded thought won't work, I find it helpful to reflect on the instruction given in the introduction to the Course lessons: *"Remember only this; you need not believe the ideas, you need not accept them, and you need not even welcome them. Some them you may actively resist. None of this will matter, or decrease their efficacy."* Then I remember that my job is only to apply these loving ideas, get out of the way and receive. As I allow the Holy Spirit to dissolve the ego's barriers I have put up in my mind,

my awareness of my Source becomes clearer. As your defenses
and fears around God come down, your acceptance of your
True Self will get easier. They go hand in hand.

*"**Spirit** is the Thought of God which He created like Himself. The unified spirit is God's one Son, or Christ."*
~ Clarification of Terms – 1.1:3-4

It is stated very clearly in the Course that our true state is
formless. We are a Thought of God, formless Mind and Spirit
together as one. What you presently believe you are, a body, is
actually a totally neutral device used for communication. You
can use your body to communicate either the ego's thoughts
or the Holy Spirit's. Try not to be deceived by the limits of the
body. It is a tool to be used lovingly and does not represent
what you really are. Your experience of the body will be useful
for the time required for you to reach enlightenment, either in
this physical experience or one to come. Then, you will lay it
aside and your formless state will go on as It always has.

True Denial

Your innocence is your greatest strength, as there is no
power in guilt. Acknowledging your innocence brings your
mind above the insecurity, pettiness and conflict of the ego
realm. When you remind yourself of your innocence, you come
into alignment with *how* your Source knows you to truly be.
Every time you mistakenly delve into the ego's thought system,
you have forgotten yourself. A question you can ask yourself
is; *"How can I remember God if I keep investing in the ego's
opinion of me?"*

The most powerful mental stance you can take in this

experience is not to let the ego affect you. This is called True Denial and Right-Minded thinking depends upon it. As you know, Right-Mindedness leads to One-Mindedness, which means True Denial is required in order for you to remember your Oneness with your Source. I rely upon True Denial whenever I recognize I'm giving in to ego thoughts. If you begin your day by putting your Higher Self in charge and are committed to choosing peace, True Denial will help you maintain that Right-Minded position. Whenever an ego thought creeps in, you can simply remind yourself that the ego cannot affect you if you so choose and you withdraw your belief in the mistaken thought. I used True Denial when I felt magnetized to the bed, couch or floor due to vertigo. Unable to open my eyes or move comfortably, I reminded myself that I have a choice in how I think. What was happening with my body did not have to dictate how I think.

If you remind yourself that only what Source created is true and nothing else is true, the ego loses its stranglehold on your mind. Source did not make my body and Source did not make vertigo – I did. If I made it, then I can change my mind about these things which I made. That's true power. This may sound shocking, but the Course asserts that we have the power to raise the dead. As we made the idea of death ourselves, we can change our minds about it. That's how powerful our minds really are.

In the Course, it is taught that True Denial is a powerful protective device for your mind that keeps you from delving into the ego. During those hours of vertigo when I couldn't open my eyes or move comfortably, it would have been so easy to say everything was going wrong. During any worldly trial, it can be easy to give in to the drama because we're used to doing so. Applying True Denial comes from a place within you where you see you don't want the pain anymore. You recognize that you do have to think differently so you can respond to the world differently. Instead of giving in, you can step back and see you don't have to play the ego's game anymore. That's the freedom True Denial gives you.

During one vertigo session, I asked Eric to turn on one of my key ingredients for good mental health, the television show 'America's Funniest Home Videos.' I couldn't watch the show but I could listen to it. Friendly laughter always cuts through the ego's seriousness and makes implementing True Denial easier. Loving humour is a great reminder that we don't have to take this world so seriously. Denying what the ego had to say about the vertigo brought me to a peaceful place in my mind and helped me remember that God is my Reality. The benefits of remembering your Source await your decision. This is all done in the privacy of your own mind and so you are safe to apply True Denial any time. Your inner peace relies upon it. Once you forget the ego through True Denial, you are able to remember God.

Communicating with God

> *"Remember always that you cannot be anywhere except in the Mind of God."* ~ T.9.VIII.5:3

Right now, you are at Home in the Mind of God. Because of this fact, communicating with your Source should be natural for you. Presently though, your preoccupation with the ego's ramblings is distracting you from realizing this is true. The lessons in the Course train your mind to become comfortable with the quality of peace that only a connection with your Source can bring. The moments of connection you can have with your Source are invaluable to your mental health. In many of the Course lessons, we are invited to close our eyes and momentarily forget the happenings of the world so we can remember God. I have found that doing this gives me the confidence to choose peace when I open my eyes and begin functioning in the world again.

True Prayer

Communicating with God is known in the Course as True Prayer. Like most teachings in the Course, it is vastly different than the kind of prayers we're used to. Instead of asking for things or thinking you need something, True Prayer requires that you remember Where and What you really are and recognize that in Reality, you have no needs and no concerns. A beautiful part of True Prayer is accepting that you are perfectly loved and cared for by your Source right now, in this moment and every moment. This is far different than the ego's form of prayer, which always comes from a place of lack and suffering. The ego's form of prayer only reinforces the separation that you believe exists between you and your Source. It keeps you focused on trying to fix the world instead of mentally rising above it. As you know, if you continue to focus on the problem, you are in the ego mind and will only get more of the problem. True Prayer is a way of forgetting your issues and remembering the Truth.

True Prayer is outlined in a supplement to the Course known as the Song of Prayer pamphlet. Within it, we are given direct guidance on what is required to communicate with our Source. This means leaving our worries and goals in the care of the Holy Spirit, thus clearing our minds for some undistracted time with Source. It is essential you realize that connecting with your Source involves a complete letting go, if even for a short amount of time, of all that you think you need. What this does for you is the alignment of your mind with Spirit. Consequently, you may receive inspiration which can help you with your earthly needs and concerns.

> *"We take our wandering thoughts, and gently bring them back to where they fall in line with all the thoughts we share with God."* ~ Lesson 188

As someone who uses True Prayer frequently, I can say that the beauty of this practice is in letting go of fear and feeling completely safe. For all that we face in this world, it really is a gift to feel perfectly cared for and safe for a few minutes. You can expect to feel relief, which I always find leads to a strong feeling of gratitude. When you feel untouchable by the ego, you can't help but feel immensely grateful that the Truth is true and nothing else is true. I often find myself thanking my Source for creating me and for the illusion being just that: an illusion.

> *"It is quite possible to listen to God's Voice all through the day without interrupting your regular activities in any way. The part of your mind in which truth abides is in constant communication with God, whether you are aware of it or not."* ~ Lesson 49

Connecting with your Source doesn't have to be a fussy ordeal. It's meant to be a time of peace where you open your mind. Isn't it a joyful thing to know that you don't have to focus on your grievances or problems? Isn't it nice to have permission to be innocent, peaceful and trusting in Spirit? These are some of the gifts True Prayer gives you. With practice, your confidence will grow as you come to see that you can let go of your concerns and know that you are still safe.

You can think of it this way: Whatever is part of your script is going to occur. This is not to scare you, but to show that you always have an opportunity to strengthen your mind. Whatever you may encounter, it is your thoughts about it which adorn the experience either with fear or peace. When down with vertigo or frozen in a panic attack, I knew I didn't need to add fear thoughts to the experience. I saw it was best to deepen my breathing, quiet my mind and just let the experience flow. Through doing so, you can align with the Holy Spirit which will always lead you directly to the peace of God. All things will pass; you just have to let them.

We are taught in the Course that the peace of God is our inheritance. The practice of True Prayer highlights that peace really is possible, no matter what seems to be occurring. It requires training your mind to get there but it is doable. Just as you can think with the ego, you can think peacefully as well. Every experience will come to teach you this in time – why not learn it now?

> *"God is your safety in every circumstance. His Voice speaks for Him in all situations and in every aspect of all situations, telling you exactly what to do to call upon His strength and His protection. There are no exceptions because God has no exceptions."* ~ Lesson 47

Enlightenment

"Heaven is not a place nor a condition. It is merely an awareness of perfect Oneness, and the knowledge that there is nothing else; nothing outside this Oneness, and nothing else within." ~ T.18.VI.1:5-6

Enlightenment truly is possible for me and for you. Not only is it possible, it's actually essential. Your commitment to healing your mind is the greatest gift you can give to yourself and others, and is also a way of being in service to Spirit. The healing of your mind is incredibly important. *You* are important. You are a fundamental part of the God Mind and deserve peace.

"Enlightenment is a recognition and not a change at all." ~ Lesson 188

I always like to remind my clients when they feel overwhelmed or deflated by the world that they can remember they are already enlightened – they're already Home. This is another teaching from the Course that can be seen as radical: the mass illusion is already healed. It was done the instant the tiny, mad idea seemed to occur. It just doesn't seem that way because if we were to experience the entirety of our physical experiences at once, it would be too much for us to be consciously aware of. So time is laid out like a red carpet where we experience physicality in a linear fashion. Our present experience is really just a replay of what has already gone by. Each moment we are choosing which version of our script we want to replay – ego's version or the Holy Spirit's version.

I've always found it comforting to know we've already healed. Celebrate and be joyful because you did it! All you really need do now is choose for the Holy Spirit's version of your script, which will expedite your experience of enlightenment. Just like we are taught in the Course, be vigilant only for God and Its Kingdom. It's your Home and you deserve to be there.

"God's more basic law; that love creates itself, and nothing but itself." ~ T.25.III.1:6

One of the Course lessons is that God's Will for us is perfect happiness. It's okay to enjoy the things of this world. It's just a dream and if you stay Right-Minded about it, you're going to enjoy the dream even more. Every day I am grateful that I get to commit to joy. It's what my Source wants for me and after everything I've gone through in my thirties, it's genuinely what I want for me too. Whenever I feel a bit anxious or concerned, I remind myself that God wants me to be happy so I really can let the fear go. I often check myself by saying that the ego doesn't get to win anymore. Not that it's a competition, but Holy Spirit is the One Who I'm doing things with now, and I feel fear dissolve pretty quickly when I declare this. Happiness is your gateway to God.

"The mind returns to its proper function only when it wills to know." ~ T.3.IV.5:6

After reading this section, you may or may not realize that you are capable of becoming enlightened and connecting with your Source. Try not to overthink what is possible; you don't have to force this. When trying to remember where you left your keys, at some point you just recall where they are. This is more easily done when your mind is relaxed. There are things I have mentioned which you can do to relax your mind and undo the ego in your mind which is your real block to remembering God:

- Turn to H.S. when you need help and stop going it alone.
- Connect with your Source. Simply say hello in the morning, then quiet your mind if even for a minute to feel love and safety.
- With each ego hiccup, apply True Denial and remind yourself of Who you really are. Be vigilant only for God and Its Kingdom which is your Home.
- Try to remind yourself that you cannot know your Source if you are in an ego-state, holding onto grievances and feeling anxious about what may or may not happen.

If you are happy, loving, forgiving, kind, and peaceful, you are expressing God's immense Love. You may not feel this way all the time, and it's okay to feel upset sometimes. You just don't want to stay there. Let yourself move through your anger, sadness, or pain, and you will get to a better mental place the sooner you stop fighting the experience. There is no rule as to how long a trial should last. God is always there and you're not doing anything wrong by moving through the emotions of this world. As I like to say, keep the door to the Holy Spirit ajar. You may not always feel like forgiving or being peaceful, but you can let yourself get there. This is about not perpetuating the ego's agenda. Even if you do, you can forgive yourself and move on.

One of the greatest lessons PTSD has taught me is to stop fussing about this world and start enjoying the eternal present moment. We are taught in the Course that God created us to create the good, the beautiful and the holy. You are *fully* supported by Spirit in doing that which makes you feel peaceful and happy. As a Child of God, You deserve it. Through everything you seem to face, you can remember God.

A little bit more about your mind...

Before we delve into the laws of the mind, there is just a bit more helpful information you should know about your mind. This information will highlight the different levels which your mind seems to operate within the split-mind experience. These levels have no relevance at the level of the One Mind.

Decision-Maker

Your greatest power in this physical experience is your ability to decide. As you know, you can only ever choose between the Holy Spirit and the ego. Kenneth Wapnick taught that the decision-maker is the ego's greatest enemy because it is the part of your mind which can decide against the ego, thus snuffing it out. This is an important topic and I will be elaborating on the decision-maker mind in a later chapter.

Conscious Mind

The conscious mind is a level of awareness. You are in the level of the conscious mind most of the time throughout your waking day. In the Course, it is referred to as the mind of action. It is an important level because it is where you are able to notice your patterns, behaviours and the thoughts you are choosing to act upon. You hold great power at the conscious level because it is where you can choose for the ego or the Holy Spirit.

This level of the mind can become quite an agitated state

if your mind is untrained. The corresponding brainwave level for the conscious mind is Beta which is activated when you are analyzing and judging. When your mind is untrained, you are doing these things too much and this can lead you to feel anxious and edgy. As mentioned though, you do have the power at the conscious level to choose to chill out. It is at this level of the mind that you will be doing your mind training work where you catch yourself thinking with the ego mind and switch over to your Right Mind.

Subconscious Mind

The subconscious mind is more of an inward experience, a part of your mind which drives your habit systems and conditioned responses. You are in your subconscious mind when you are fantasizing or deeply focused on any visualization, when you are in a hypnotic trance, and also when you are in the beginning stages of sleep. The benefit of being in your subconscious mind is that you are more relaxed as the ego mind is more subdued. This makes hearing Spirit's guidance easier for you and this is why you are encouraged in the exercises of A Course in Miracles to practice quieting your mind more often as it is when your mind is quiet that you can receive the inspiration of Spirit which is always available to you.

As a reminder, all answers come to a quiet mind, so there is great benefit to creating a practice of calming your mind. Deep breathing is an excellent conduit for a peaceful mind.

Unconscious Mind

The unconscious mind has been mentioned quite a bit so far and this is because it is the largest part of your mind which houses the ego as well as the memory of God. It carries all the information from all your lifetime experiences (including experiences which appear to happen in the future). This means that the information housed in your unconscious mind fuels the content you experience with your subconscious and conscious minds.

Due to the ego being housed in this part of your mind, this is where the Holy Spirit does Its work. Your job is at the conscious mind level where you actively choose for the Holy Spirit. The Holy Spirit's job is to undo the ego at the level of your unconscious mind. So, you want to invite the Holy Spirit in to do just that, which is how you will remember God.

In Gary Renard's work, it is highlighted how sensitive the unconscious mind is. We are taught that at this level, the mind knows there is only one of us and therefore takes all judgements we make and accepts them as being messages about ourselves. I will be sharing more about this and its importance in your mental health and ultimate enlightenment.

CHAPTER FOUR

The Laws of the Mind

"The outstanding characteristics of the laws of the mind as they operate in this world is that by obeying them, and I assure you that you must obey them, you can arrive at diametrically opposed results." ~ T.7.II.2:8

As *PI* is fundamental to every curve in the universe, the following laws are fundamental to your mind. As *A Course in Miracles* is really a course in mind training, it makes sense that it would offer the laws which govern the mind. Some of these laws may be obvious and others may be new to you. Some will only be relevant while you are in the dream and others outline how you, as a Child of Source, came to be without ever leaving your Source.

Because you are mind itself, these laws outline how *you* function. By understanding these laws, you will be able to clearly see how you've contributed to the state of your mind and what you can do to improve it. The importance of doing so is that by improving your state of mind, you are able to undo the ego and accept your Source and your True Identity again.

I have recognized these laws within the teachings of spiritual texts like the Tao Te Ching and in the works of Abraham-Hicks, Louise Hay, Deepak Chopra, and others. I am confident

that many spiritual students, no matter the message and mes-
sengers they resonate with, will be attracted to these laws and
find them to be true.

Remember that the ego doesn't have exclusive rights to
your mind and its laws. The laws reveal that whatever thought
you choose to take seriously will be reinforced, so it may be
helpful for you to be pickier about the thoughts you enter-
tain. I have personally found that my awareness of the laws of
the mind has helped me develop my trust in thinking Right-
Mindedly.

The laws of the mind also highlight our inherent connection. Behind the physical façade of the body and the unique
circumstances of our individual lives and experiences, we are
fundamentally the same. In the Course, we are taught that
healing occurs among equals. You are not better or less than
others, you are perfectly equal to them. We are all one in the
Mind of God, it just appears that we are having different experiences and have different perceptions, but that is not a reason
to ever see inequality. Seen through the laws of the mind, the
smoke screen of separateness clears away. As you will come
to see, all those who appear 'out there' in the world are really
'in there' – in your mind. How you view them is how you keep
yourself in a personal hell of fear or release yourself and them
in peace. Remember, separation does not exist. The laws of the
mind will help you to see that this is true.

LAW #1 – *The Law of Cause and Effect*

*"There are no idle thoughts. All thinking produces form
at some level."* ~ T.2.VI.9:13-14

The law of cause and effect is the most fundamental. Although this law appears to describe two different phenomena, *cause* and *effect* are actually one. This is because the effect exists only because of the cause, thus giving cause its identity. Without cause there would be no effect; likewise without an effect, cause would not exist. Thus they are one. In the Course, Jesus states for us not to ask him to save us from fear because that would be interjecting on this fundamental law of the mind. We experience fear because we believed in a fear thought. Jesus continues by stating that it's far more effective to reinforce the power of our minds so we don't misuse them for the ego's purposes and feel fear.

Mind is the level of cause, always. In this physical experience, your mind is the cause and the physical projection of your body and its sensations, along with emotions, are all effects. For example: When you believe in a fear thought and suddenly feel visceral discomfort, that physical reaction is an effect. In our world, it is more common to address the physical discomfort of our thoughts than it is to address and correct the thoughts which led to the uncomfortable effect. Ideally, if you use something to alleviate physical discomfort, you want to be sure to use forgiveness as well so the real cause of your discomfort is corrected.

At the level of the One Mind, the Mind of God is Cause and we, the Child of God, are the Effect. Remember that we, the Child of God, are described as being a Thought of God. Because cause and effect are one, we are fundamentally one with our Source. And because of cause and effect, the world which seems outside of us is actually being projected from our minds and is an effect. As is so clearly emphasized in the Course, our perception of the world is the result of an inward condition.

The ego's plan is to convince us that the world is outside us. This leaves us feeling that we are victims of the world, vulnerable and afraid of what could possibly happen to us. To believe we are prey to a world outside of us is a 'thought reversal' wherein the effect (the world) seems to be the cause. This confusion is the cause of sickness, endowing the body with creative, causative power it doesn't actually have. The world and your body are effects of your mind. If you believe you are just a body, then you won't recognize you are really mind and have the power to change all the investments of your belief. Mistakenly believing you are prey to the effect keeps you caught in the dream.

"This self he sees as being acted on, reacting to external forces as they demand, and helpless midst the power of the world." ~ Process of Psychotherapy–1–3.6

The Course addresses thought reversal by reminding you that you are the 'dreamer of the dream.' Until you know that you are the dreamer, you will remain stuck within the dream believing it's all real. How can you wake up from a dream if you don't know you are dreaming? Or, how can you realize your mind is the cause if you think its effect is the cause? As the dreamer, you have the ability to choose to wake up, which can only be done by acknowledging that your mind is the cause.

Now, you don't want to carry the entire state of the world and other people's vicious behaviour on your shoulders. The world and the entire universe are a product of the collective mind, appearing to be billions of separate minds having separate bodily experiences. **You are responsible for your**

perception – your part of the dream. Recognizing cause means that you recognize your own reactions and your participation in the ego's agenda. You see that you are no longer a victim and can choose to withdraw ego thoughts from any and all situations.

> *"This is a crucial step in dealing with illusions. No one is afraid of them when he perceives he made them up. The fear was held in place because he did not see that he was author of the dream, and not a figure in the dream."* ~ T.28.II.7:2-4

The effects of Love are a healthy perspective and a relaxed body. In fact, it is stated in the Course that we are not meant to feel the body at all, so as you begin to dis-identify from the ego, you can expect not to feel the heaviness of bodily identification. The effects of Love are totally benign, warranting no judgment and thus supporting a peaceful state of mind.

CHAPTER FIVE

LAW OF THE MIND #2
The Law of Free Will

"Free will must lead to freedom."
~ T.3.VII.11:3

THIS divine law states that each of us has the right to decide what we think and believe. The split mind experiences the law of free will as feeling free to make our own decisions and have our own points of view. At the level of the One Mind, the law of free will enables you to experience the joy of creating all that is perfect. In this sense, your free will is a beautiful gift and an extension of your Source's love for you.

You exercise your free will all the time. The thoughts you take seriously, the opinions you accept as true, and the beliefs you hold are all enabled by your free will. There may have been times in your life when you felt that someone forced their beliefs upon you; this is a common experience, especially when we are young and developing. Now that you are older, you are able to be pickier about the ideas you accept as true. In the face of the ego and other people's opinions, it's comforting to remember that you have free will and can believe what you will. What is real for you in your own mind is not the responsibility of anyone else.

At the ego level, we can get easily lost in the game of blaming others and external circumstances for our troubles. To do this is a reversal in cause and effect, mistakenly placing responsibility for your state of mind on external factors. If you do so, you are using both the law of cause and effect and the law of free will against yourself. This keeps you stuck in the dream. To remember you have free will helps you change your mind about how you perceive all things, including past painful memories and future concerns. This recognition helps you open up to the Holy Spirit's True Perception. Exercising your free will is how you will maintain a Right-Minded state, and is essential to your application of True Denial: the truth that the ego cannot affect you.

One of my favourite examples of free will being used correctly is from Viktor Frankl, author of *Man's Search for Meaning*. In his book, Frankl shares that "Everything can be taken from a man but one thing, the last of the human freedoms — To choose one's attitude in any given set of circumstances, to choose one's own way." This was a man who faced the Nazis while surviving a concentration camp. Even he was able to see that he alone was in charge of his own thinking, even in the midst of the most challenging temptations to blame.

Your free will is always honoured by the spiritual realm. As spiritual students, it can be tempting to wonder why this world was allowed to happen, or why didn't Spirit just wake us up from the illusion. The law of free will states that nothing, not even Spirit, can intervene in your decisions. For all you Star Trek fans, it is like the Prime Directive, where a more advanced race cannot interfere with the evolution of another race, upholding the free will of all species and the rate at which they learn and evolve. We must have a willingness and a desire to see things differently before the Holy Spirit can get involved. This allows us to recognize our mistakes and learn to make a different and loving choice.

You are allowed to be choosy about the thoughts you harbour. You can be much more vigilant for the Holy Spirit and decide against the ego. It is your free will that got you into the dream, and it is your free will that will get you out.

CHAPTER SIX

LAW OF THE MIND #3
Ideas Leave Not Their Source

*"...ideas leave not their source. If this is true, how can you
be apart from God? How could you walk the world alone
and separate from your Source?" ~ Lesson 156.1:3-5*

Now we have creation's law: Ideas leave not their source.
This law explains that we are one with our Source because all thoughts or ideas begin in the mind, and it is there
they remain. As we are a Thought of God, it is in the Mind
of God where we remain. This can be a very comforting law
to remember especially when you feel alone or helpless. The
strength of God is with you at all times because of this wonderful law.

*"And none (thought) can leave the thinker's mind, or
leave him unaffected." ~ T.21.VII.13:8*

Within the separated mind experience, this law means
that you are never apart from the judgements you make nor
are you immune to the effects of your thinking. In our society,
the ability to judge others is glorified. The quicker you can cut
someone down, the smarter and tougher you are thought to
be. Yet the misuse of this law is what fuels our emotional pain
because you are actually not immune to your own judgments.

Every time you judge another, or project onto them, you have just reinforced what exists in your mind. You have not escaped from your judgements at all.

Perhaps you've noticed that you feel low energy or in a bad mood at times when your judgments are strong. Jesus teaches in his Course that the reason we are fatigued at the end of the day is because of all the judgements we've made. The ego will tell you that you're safe to make judgements of others, and even that your survival depends on judgment. It's how the ego, or fear, functions.

"Guilt is inevitable in those who use their judgment in making their decisions. Guilt is impossible in those through whom the Holy Spirit speaks." ~ Purpose of Psychotherapy.VII.4:6-7

I find it helpful to think of our thoughts in this way: Loving thoughts and creative ideas are like balloons floating gently and peacefully around you. Ego judgements are like weights dragging you down. What's worse is that we have to maintain our judgements in order to validate them in our minds. Spirit, on the other hand, would advise you to just let the judgments go.

It is essential to our peace of mind that we remember this fundamental law of the mind. You want to be picky about the thoughts you hold and the judgments you make, for they stay with you. In *A Course in Miracles* it is taught that we can lay the heaviness of our judgments aside *"...not with regret but with a sigh of gratitude. Now are you free of a burden so great that you could merely stagger and fall down beneath it."* ~ Manual for Teachers:10:5.1-2

CHAPTER SEVEN

LAW OF THE MIND #4

The Law of Decision

*"The power of decision is your one remaining freedom
as a prisoner of this world. You can decide to see it right."*

~ T.12.VII.9:1-2

To DECIDE is the exercise of free will. Whether you realize it or not, you are frequently deciding whether to play the ego's game or step back and connect with the Holy Spirit. As you have learned, there is no other choice available to you. No matter how trivial a choice seems, your decision will represent what you think you are: the ego or a Child of God. Therefore, your decisions either perpetuate the illusion or bring you to the experience of the Truth.

"The mind is the mechanism of decision."
~ T. 12.III.9:10

As long as you decide for the ego, your mind will remain untrained – and as we are taught in the Course, an untrained mind can accomplish nothing. This law of the mind declares that we are not victims but decision makers. We are responsible for our thoughts, beliefs, words, and actions. We make decisions and have complete control over our minds. It only seems like the ego controls our thinking because we have afforded the ego the power of our belief. It is only because we keep deciding for the ego that it seems real. When we accept that we are the decision makers for our own minds, we begin to recognize that we are no longer the victims we thought ourselves to be.

> *"...our experience in the world of 'hearing' two voices or thought systems: I can release this grievance and be happy, or hold onto it and be miserable – and I am aware of both possibilities."* ~ Ken Wapnick, *Journey through the Manual for Teachers*

You are able to freely choose how you think without being dependent upon external circumstances or influences. To choose for the Holy Spirit no matter what you seem to face will become your greatest strength. It is a Right-Minded habit you can create. If you are in a challenging situation, you don't need to force happiness, but you can let yourself get there by not choosing for the ego. This is something I have shared before but is worth repeating. You can stop the cycle of ego thinking and let your mind relax to feel your experiences without any ego commentary.

Once you make a decision, your mind will follow that trajectory until a new decision is made. As your mind quiets and the uncomfortable energy passes, you can then genuinely decide for the Holy Spirit. With practice, choosing for the Holy Spirit will become your immediate decision when faced with any upset. Inner peace begins with your decision to stop thinking with the ego.

In the Course, Jesus shares that it was awareness of his decisions which led him to become enlightened. *"It was only my decision that gave me all power in Heaven and earth"* ~ T.5.II.9. This is a very powerful statement. You will not know what you are truly capable of as long as you choose for the ego's weakness. Imagine the miracles which await your decision for the Holy Spirit. This is why I encourage you to begin your day by connecting with the Holy Spirit, a decision which lessens the guilt in your mind because it chooses for unity which is always healing, not separation which always leads to suffering. You can open your mind to the Holy Spirit's guidance by simply saying, *"Today I will make no decisions by myself"* ~ T.30.I.2:2. A world of miracles awaits your decision.

> *"It is still up to you to choose to join with truth or with illusion. But remember that to choose one is to let the other go. Which one you choose you will endow with beauty and reality, because the choice depends on which you value more. The spark of beauty or the veil of ugliness, the real world or the world of guilt and fear, truth or illusion, freedom or slavery-it is all the same. For you can never choose except between God and the ego."* ~ T.17.IV.9.1-4

CHAPTER EIGHT

LAW OF THE MIND #5
The Law of Perception

"You see what you believe is there, and you believe it there
because you want it there. Perception has no other law
than this." ~ T.25.III.1:3-4

PERCEPTION is only experienced within the split mind and has nothing to do with the Knowledge of the One Mind. The ego misuses perception by bringing the mind into a questioning state where it has to choose how it wants to see. In the Course, we are taught that only our perception can be sick and so it is our perception which needs to be corrected so healing of the mind can occur. As examples, things like physical illness or unhealthy eco-systems, are effects of unconscious guilt in the individual or collective minds. The True Perception of the Holy Spirit can only lead to the God Mind, thus it is the correction we need to the ego's version of perception.

Our perception acts as a filter for how we perceive what seems to be outside of us. You can perceive either with the ego or you can use the Holy Spirit's True Perception. Once a decision is made as to which mind to perceive with, the wrong mind or Right Mind, you then perceive the witnesses to your decision outside of you.

*"Perception is a choice of what you want yourself
to be; the world you want to live in, and the state in
which you think your mind will be content and satis-
fied."* ~ T.25.I.3:1

Which kind of perception you choose leads to how you experience yourself. Your self-image is a perception; the thoughts
you have repeated through all these years have led you to perceive yourself the way you presently do. This also goes for your
surroundings. No matter how peaceful and beautiful your surroundings may be, none of it will matter if your perception is
ego-based.

For example, my parents moved to Canada to escape the
civil war in Northern Ireland known as 'the troubles.' Although
they had moved to a peaceful environment, their mental states
had been traumatized from the war. Their perceptions were
skewed and it took some time for them to grow accustomed to
their new surroundings and develop new perceptions of being
comfortable. No matter where you go in this world, your state
of mind based on your perceptions will follow you everywhere.

With every thought you take seriously, you strengthen
your perception. Therefore you want to become aware of how
often you are choosing and reinforcing the ego's perception, so
you can begin to make the switch over to the Holy Spirit's True
Perception. Until you choose for the Holy Spirit, the ego's perception will reinforce separation in your mind, strengthening
unnecessary guilt.

*"And it is given you to make a different choice, and
use perception for a different purpose. And what you
see will serve that purpose well, and prove its own*

reality to you." ~ T.24.VII.11:12-13

Correct use of perception develops trust in the Holy Spirit. It is taught in the Course that when we are caught in the world of perception we are caught in a dream. The only way out of the dream is to perceive differently. Specifically, as you choose for the Holy Spirit's version of reality, you will begin to see this world in a more loving way and your mind will come to be peaceful and benign. The Course teaches that the world you see is a picture of an inward condition. If you want to see peace, you must choose for peace. This is how you will break the habit of perceiving with the ego.

"Peace of mind is clearly an internal matter. It must begin with your own thoughts, and then extend outward. It is from your peace of mind that a peaceful perception of the world arises." ~ Lesson 34

CHAPTER NINE

LAW OF THE MIND #6
Your Mind is Only Ever Projecting or Extending

"Every mind must project or extend, because that is how it lives, and every mind is life." ~ T.7.VIII.1:11

Y OU have learned that we are an Effect of the Mind of God. Through this law we learn that we were created through extension from this Mind. Love always extends into eternity. For this reason, love is never lost nor wasted. The ego has its own version of extension which is known as projection. Specifically, love extends and fear projects. Projection is the ego's attempt to get rid of something it does not want. Extension is Source's way of creating. Through extension or projection is how your mind functions.

Within the split-mind experience, projection is common. As a reminder, projection is a way of attempting to get rid of the guilt which causes all your suffering. Through the ego's eyes, we can get rid of our guilt by seeing it in someone else. This is a mental trap which only strengthens the idea of guilt in your mind. Remember, ideas leave not their source. For this reason, your attempts to project onto someone or something else are never successful.

As this law states, your mind is always either projecting or extending, but it cannot do both at the same time. You can't be in both thought systems at one time; they are mutually exclusive. The mind is fully capable of shifting thought systems, which is positive news. Know that just because an ego thought crept up and momentarily shook you, you do not have to continue thinking that way. To shift out of ego-mode, here is a helpful teaching from the Course you can use:

> *"In all these diversionary tactics, however, the one question that is never asked by those who pursue them is, 'What for?' This is the question that you must learn to ask in connection with everything. What is the purpose? Whatever it is, it will direct your efforts automatically. When you make a decision of purpose, then, you have made a decision about your future effort; a decision that will remain in effect unless you change your mind."* ~ T.4.V.6:7-11

When you follow the guidance in the above quote, you will find that the question *"What for?"* will remind you that the ego is trying to steal your focus from the Truth while the Holy Spirit is nudging you to be Right-Minded. Projection is an attempt to make someone feel guilty, and extension will always honour someone's inherent innocence. You can easily view anything and anyone, including yourself, through your Right Mind. As you know, that is a matter of decision on your part.

What is also helpful for you to realize is that when you make a decision, you can't just have a little of the thought system you have chosen. There is no grey area between the ego and the Holy Spirit. For example: If you say you like someone but you will never forgive them for a certain mistake, then you have not fully chosen the thought system of love. You have held onto a block to love, and that choice is all or nothing. You can't have a little ego and a little Spirit at the same time. Understanding that you choose only to project or extend – choosing ego or choosing the Holy Spirit – will make it easier to choose for sanity. This law reinforces the awareness that you are always choosing either the wrong mind or your Right Mind.

CHAPTER TEN

LAW OF THE MIND #7

Thoughts Increase by Being Shared

"To study the error itself does not lead to correction,
if you are indeed to succeed in overlooking the error."
~ Clarification of Terms – Introduction – 1:5

THIS law is the foundation of perception: Every thought you give attention to is strengthened in your mind. This is how fear grows stronger, but this law can also be the key to correcting your thoughts with greater ease. Used correctly, this law helps you to accept the Holy Spirit's True Perception undoing the ego in your mind, and leads to remembering your True Identity. Used incorrectly, this law makes you the silent investor in your own fear.

Jesus shares in his Course that *we cannot afford a negative thought*. If we can't even afford a negative thought, then just think of the mental detriment of repeating them. We repeat our thoughts in many ways, some of which are quite subtle. Worrying, analyzing a topic, or even seeking reassurance when you're afraid are some of those ways. Without correction, negative thoughts will be repeated and become part of your perception.

For example: I met a teenage girl and her mother at a book signing for my first children's book, *My Mind Book*. The mother was very interested in how the book's teachings could help her daughter out of her anxiety. Her daughter was specifically afraid that a python or anaconda would move up through the heat vent in their home and smother her while she was in the shower. As an initial defense to help the daughter remain calm, they resorted to having a family member stay in the bathroom with her while she showered. Once the family tired of this tactic, they decided that she would remain in the bathroom alone and suggested she put her clothes over the vent so a man-eating snake couldn't enter the bathroom. The mother admitted that this had been going on for months and she was at a loss as to what to do. The situation worsened because a correction in thinking like True Forgiveness or practicing non-judgement of the fear thought, was not applied and fear thoughts were repeated.

It is common for us to feel helpless when experiencing the endless stream of fear thoughts which invades our minds. *A Course in Miracles* teaches that fear binds the world which is only because we repeat fear thoughts and act from them. We must recognize that we are active participants in our own fear. Remember that nothing is being done *to* us, it's all being done *by* us. The decision about which thoughts we share, and the frequency with which we do so, is a key part in how long we experience fear. We are the ones who initially believe in a fear thought, giving it life in our minds. Without taking the time to correct the fear thought, we will unintentionally repeat it.

To use this law of the mind correctly you must be mindful of the ideas and stories you share with others or repeat to yourself. *A Course in Miracles* provides a mental exercise for this awareness:

"When anything seems to you to be a source of fear, when any situation strikes you with terror and makes your body tremble and the cold sweat of fear comes over it, remember it is always for one reason, the ego has perceived it as a symbol of fear, a sign of sin and death... Confronted with such seeming uncertainty of meaning, judge it not. Remember the holy Presence of the One given to you to be the Source of judgment. Give it to Him to judge for you, and say:

'Take this from me and look upon it, judging it for me. Let me not see it as a sign of sin and death, nor use it for destruction. Teach me how not to make of it an obstacle to peace, but Let You use it for me, to facilitate its (peace) coming.'" ~ T.19.IV.C.i.11:1/5-10

It's also helpful to have one or two people you trust to whom you can turn when you're feeling overwhelmed or hurt. It's okay to vent or share a story so that someone can understand how to support you. You don't have to keep things pent up inside; you just want to be mindful of repeating stories to strengthen them. A person you trust can help you feel understood and cared for while also empowering your capacity to heal. Of course, you always have the love and guidance of the Holy Spirit available.

As the gatekeeper to your mind, you are in charge of the thoughts you share and you actively decide how long fear grips your mind. The repetition of fear thoughts for the ego's purposes prevents you from attaining inner peace. You must forget the ego in order to remember the Truth. From a peaceful frame of mind, you can share the thoughts which represent the Truth

in our world. Thoughts of peace and True Forgiveness are worthy of being repeated. Also, creative thoughts which bring you
joy are also worth sharing. Repeating loving thoughts will help
you to feel calm and joyful, making it much easier for you to be
Right-Minded whenever a trial begins.

CHAPTER ELEVEN

LAW OF THE MIND #8
Fidelity to Your Beliefs

THIS law of the mind states that we are loyal to our beliefs. This may seem obvious but it's important to realize how our loyalty to unhealthy beliefs can sabotage our inner peace. We are loyal to the "laws" of chaos and all the ego beliefs which uphold chaos, simply because we made them.

Belief is very powerful. The repetition of thoughts forms them into beliefs that stabilize your perception. At this point on your spiritual journey, it would be helpful to observe where you are investing your beliefs. The Course offers us a complete reversal in our thinking, bringing us to question the value and relevancy of our beliefs. As long as you want to remain loyal to the ego, your style of perception cannot transform into True Perception. This leads us to the ever-important topic of willingness, required in order to see with the Holy Spirit. You must be willing to see things differently, beginning with a willingness to let go of what you are presently loyal to.

"No evidence will convince you of the truth of what you do not want." ~ T.16.II.6:1

If we are not ready to accept a new truth, then that's simply where we are at that point. We are not ready to relinquish our loyalty to how we presently think. It's okay not to be ready; no one feels good being forced to something they don't believe or understand. What I have found is that the Holy Spirit helps me get to the point where I suddenly grasp a spiritual concept. This always happens when I have asked for help in understanding something. The Holy Spirit is your own Higher Self, so you're not going to feel pressured into accepting something you're not ready for. One day you have an 'Aha!' moment and you just get it.

This transformation in your thinking is a natural process; the Holy Spirit won't force anything, It will simply respond when you open up to a new way of thinking, a decision you can make either consciously or unconsciously. When the transformation happens, you are able to apply your new understanding to all areas of your life. This is because the loving change has altered the filter of your mind, your perception. The loving change becomes how you see things anew.

In the introduction to the Course Workbook, we are taught about the transfer of Right-Minded ideas to all situations and people. In your application of the lessons, you practice implementing the Holy Spirit's True Perception. We are guided not to make exceptions in applying Course lessons so that our perceptions can be healed. If you make any exceptions, your loyalty to the ego will remain, continuing to block the awareness of love's presence in your mind. Full transfer of Right-Mindedness to all that you see and experience is how your fidelity can switch from the ego to the Holy Spirit and ultimately, to God.

"The Holy Spirit can use all that you give to Him for your salvation. But He cannot use what you withhold, for He cannot take it from you without your

willingness. For if He did, you would believe He wrested it from you against your will. And so you would not learn it is your will to be without it." ~ T.25.VIII.1:1-4

CHAPTER TWELVE

LAW OF THE MIND #9
As You See Others,
You Will See Yourself

*"You cannot perpetuate an illusion about another
without perpetuating it about yourself. There is no way
out of this, because it is impossible to fragment the mind."*
~ T.7.VIII.4:1-2

THROUGH the ego mind, this law keeps you in your own mental hell. Yet, when it is used correctly through your Right Mind, this law expedites your enlightenment.

In the Course, we are taught that what we extend or project is real to us. This is why we will see ourselves as we see others: *"...you will learn what you are from what you have projected onto others, and therefore believe they are"* ~ T.7.II.3:3. Essentially, you need to believe in an idea in order to project or extend it. Once you have projected an idea, you will perceive it as real because it came from your own mind. This law of the mind is the same as saying; "As you give, you receive." It all came from you and as you know, does not leave your mind but only strengthens.

This law speaks to the sensitivity of our unconscious minds. At the unconscious level, our minds know there is only one of us. Therefore, any thought we have about another is taken by the unconscious mind as being a message about ourselves. Remember, ideas leave not their source. When you make any judgement, you are reinforcing the idea in your own mind. This is how you are negatively affected by your own perception. If you make negative judgements about others, you are poisoning your own mind and affecting your self-esteem. As the old adage goes, 'hurt people hurt.' It's a cycle of negative judgement, pain, and more judgement.

In my classes, I emphasize that the worst thing you can do for your mental health is to make and keep an enemy. If you see anyone or any group of people as your enemy, you will keep perceiving the evidence that they are indeed your enemy. So, you will continue to judge them with the ego and uphold the identification you have given them. All this does is perpetuate ego thinking in your own mind. Consequently, your opinion of yourself will also suffer. If you see others as angry, depressed or suffering in any way, you are saying that it is also possible for you to feel that way. This is an easy way to become mentally and emotionally stressed. If you see the ego in others, you are seeing the ego in yourself and you remain within the dream.

The positive side of this law is that we can move swiftly towards enlightenment by seeing the truth in others. It is written in Gary Renard's work that this is how Jesus hastened his enlightenment. He was sure to see everyone truthfully, meaning he saw the innocence behind the ego façade. No matter what he faced, he did not let the ego's agenda sway him. You can recognize this teaching throughout the Course, as Jesus is constantly encouraging us to let go of our ego opinion of others and remember their truth. You simply cannot hold thoughts of attack and conflict about someone or yourself and expect inner peace. Being vigilant for the truth will bring you the peace of mind you've longed for.

Accepting your innocence and the fact that everyone else is innocent is a process. You need to recognize what the ego is up to and remember it's just an illusion. You are able to function in the world normally and still see the truth in others. It's all done privately as no one needs to know what you are thinking in order for you to choose peace. If you need to say no to something or stand up for yourself in some regard, you are still able to acknowledge the truth behind the ego screen. You are able to do all things through your Right Mind.

Understandably, many people don't want to love someone they've been in deep conflict with. But you're not asked to love that person's ego; you're asked to love their true, innocent selves. It is the True Self which you share with them. To see the truth in them is to see it in yourself because the mind is one.

CHAPTER THIRTEEN

LAW OF THE MIND #10

True Forgiveness Heals the Mind

WITHIN this physical classroom, you have a specific purpose: to forgive. *A Course in Miracles* teaches you the process of True Forgiveness, the quickest way to your Source. The law of forgiveness overrides the law of karma, every time. If you want to hop off the cycle of karma, then you must learn to practice True Forgiveness.

In the split-mind experience, the ego's version of forgiveness always retains some conflict. The Course calls it 'forgiveness to destroy.' With this form of forgiveness, you may see yourself as being better than the person you are forgiving, or you may find yourself still afraid or distrustful of that person. The ego's version of forgiveness encourages you to see other people or external events as the reason for your anguish, focusing on the effect and not the cause. Some form of rationalization for forgiveness is required for the ego. Yet, as thoughts grow stronger with repetition, the more you rationalize or remain leery, the more you focus on the illusion and become fixated upon it. The ego's version of forgiveness ensures that you remain focused on the world so your mind is not freed at all.

True Forgiveness reflects the Atonement principle, stating that this ego illusion never happened. Through True Forgiveness, you see past the illusion and forgive yourself and others for what they *didn't* do. You have to be ready to let things go because in Reality they didn't happen, and that God's Will is stronger than the ego's will. What God created is true and what the ego made isn't; that's the core of True Forgiveness. As is written in the Preface to the Course; *"All this we must learn to forgive, not because we are being 'good' and 'charitable,' but because what we are seeing is not true."*

To begin forgiving because what you are seeing isn't true may require an initial 'leap of faith' on your part. All around you the illusion screams at you that it's real. It's helpful to know then that True Forgiveness works because it releases your mind from judging this world as if it were your reality. True Forgiveness lifts your awareness above the battleground and reminds you there is something besides the pain of the ego.

All things are worthy of True Forgiveness because all that you are forgiving stems from the ego's thought system. Some trials may appear more extreme than others, but as you learned in the chapter on the ego, the differing degrees of extremity comprise an ego ploy to keep you focused on the illusion. The ego suggests that some things are just so bad there's no way they can be healed – and that other things, like a mild disagreement, are so trivial that you don't have to forgive at all. These are deceptions. All things deserve your forgiveness because only God is true and you are a fundamental part of your Source, thus always deserving of peace.

If you actively choose not to forgive, then you are choosing to maintain conflict in your life. Left unforgiven, negative occurrences, become filters for your life. Experiences are then perceived through old, irrelevant hang-ups about the past, instead of being viewed as purposeful opportunities. Left unchecked, you are consistently distracted by past hurts. The law of forgiveness undoes this painful cycle.

A common question I get in my classes is, "What exactly am I forgiving?" To clarify, you are always forgiving the fact that you misperceived the illusion as being true. Any stab of fear, anger, sadness, and the like are your red flags to forgive. When you feel those effects, it is because you took an ego thought seriously, and that's what you need to forgive. As you develop a practice of True Forgiveness, it will be easier for you to apply it to any triggering event or personality. It may seem challenging to think you should forgive a murderer, but if you don't eventually get to that point where you can, you are imprisoning your own mind. As you forgive, all minds are healed because the mind is actually one. Through True Forgiveness you are helping heal the guilt which led to whatever event you are upset about. Remember my example in the chapter on Right-Mindedness, where a mother forgave and developed a loving mother-son relationship with the man who shot her son. There have been incredible acts of forgiveness throughout human history which can serve as profound examples for all of us.

Still, you're not going to forgive until you're ready so what you can do is prep your mind to get to that place.

"You who want peace can only find it by complete forgiveness." ~ T.1.VI.1:1

I have shared many times that forgiveness is not about ignoring your feelings or condoning things you don't agree with. It's about recognizing that each ego eruption you take seriously and don't correct festers in your own mind. Each thought of attack and conflict and every act of projection disrupts *your* peace. I like to think of True Forgiveness as a way to cleanse the palette of my mind. Through years of using it, I can't imagine my life without it. It's been vital to my peace and my development of trust in the Holy Spirit. It has been instrumental in being vigilant for my loving Source. All through PTSD and Meniere's disease, I felt strong and capable because I knew exactly what it was all for – my forgiveness.

As you begin to practice True Forgiveness, start with the little things. Let your trust in it grow. With practice, it becomes easier to apply because it simply feels right. After a while, True Forgiveness becomes like taking a shower every day. You feel so much better afterward, and a bit icky when you don't do it. You can get to the point where the ego's thought system becomes undesirable and you know you can do something positive to get out of it.

The True Forgiveness Process

The process of True Forgiveness is outlined at the very end of Chapter Five of the ACIM Text. Like all Right-Minded thoughts, it is done in the privacy of your own mind and will become quicker to apply as you get used to it. Just like connecting with the Holy Spirit or your Source, you don't have to be fussy about it. Simply take a few moments and commit to correcting your thinking. Try to realize that the few moments it will take for you to apply True Forgiveness is easier on you than holding onto fear thoughts. Personally, I like to sit in my favourite chair and close my eyes to do my True Forgiveness. I also found myself doing it while I was walking Guinness before he passed. You will find it easier to do when you are happy or relaxed. You don't have to do this through gritted teeth. Enjoy the process as it's the greatest thing you will ever do for yourself.

Here is the Course's description of True Forgiveness along with the steps:

"Decision cannot be difficult. This is obvious, if you realize that you must already have decided not to be wholly joyous if that is how you feel. Therefore, the first step in the undoing is to recognize that you actively decided wrongly, but can as actively decide otherwise. Be very firm with yourself in this, and keep yourself fully aware that the undoing process, which does not come from you, is nevertheless within you because God placed it there. Your part is merely to return your thinking to the point at which the error was made, and give it over to the Atonement in peace. Say this to yourself as sincerely as you can, remembering that the Holy Spirit will respond fully to your slightest invitation:

I must have decided wrongly, because I am not at peace.

I made the decision myself, but I can also decide otherwise.

I want to decide otherwise, because I want to be at peace.

I do not feel guilty, because the Holy Spirit will undo all the consequences of my wrong decision if I will let Him.

I choose to let Him, by allowing Him to decide for God for me." ~ T.5.VII.6:1-11

This instruction says nothing about other people or the circumstances of what you are forgiving. True Forgiveness heals your perception, your filter, and this is how you begin to see people and the world with peace. Nothing needs to happen in the outside world in order for you to forgive because the outside world is an effect of the mind. Remember, the focus should be on the cause, your mind. True Forgiveness is done within because it was within your mind that the error was made. So, all forgiveness is really self-forgiveness.

True Forgiveness can be summed as: *Correct, then connect.* Once you feel upset, you can recognize it is only because you made the mistake of taking an ego thought seriously. Upon taking responsibility for the mistake, ask the Holy Spirit to take it from you for correction. Then, you connect by applying the Atonement and reminding yourself you never left your Source. Remember that the truth will correct all errors in your mind and this is why applying the Atonement is essential. Take a final moment to connect with your Source and remember that only what God created is true and nothing else is true. This undoes the ego in your mind because 'atoning' means 'undoing.'

The True Forgiveness process states that we remind ourselves 'I do not feel guilty...' Remember that guilt is the problem. You don't need to feel guilty for believing in an ego thought; you can recognize it was just a mistake. With the Holy Spirit, mistakes are to be corrected. To the ego, mistakes are sins to be punished, keeping you in its cycle of fear and projection. Without True Forgiveness, your lessons will replay in various forms until you pay attention. Remember, it is your purpose to truly forgive. That's what your lessons in this classroom are for. As stated earlier, corrected error is the error's end. We all hear the ego; even Jesus did. You don't need to believe in it though and you don't need to feel guilty if you did believe in it. Let your investment in the ego be corrected. It really is that simple.

> *"Relationships in particular must be properly perceived, and all dark cornerstones of unforgiveness removed. Otherwise the old thought system still has a basis for return."* ~ Manual for Teachers 9.1:7-9

There is so much I can say about the importance of forgiveness, beginning with: it works. As we are personally responsible for the thoughts we choose to hold and repeat, we are equally responsible for the forgiveness of our thoughts. No one else can do this for us, but the Holy Spirit, your loving Higher Self, is ready to help you out at any moment. One of the great teachings of the Course is to let healing be. You don't need to dictate when, where or how healing occurs. If you have applied True Forgiveness, trust that a part of your unconscious mind has been healed and move on.

The benefits of your True Forgiveness practice will show up in the most unexpected ways. A year ago I took the time to forgive a painful memory involving an incident with my old Irish dance teacher which occurred twenty years ago. It wasn't anything major, but I remembered how hurt I had felt and that's reason enough to forgive. A few days after I forgave the memory, she came into a store I was in and I was suddenly face-to-face with her after twenty years! The moment I saw her, I smiled and giggled at the synchronicity. I waved at her and we had a good chat, sharing how lovely it was to see each other again. Because of True Forgiveness I was given the gift of seeing her again with fresh eyes. And now I have a more pleasant memory of her and a pretty cool story to share.

Know that sometimes you won't see any physical effects of your True Forgiveness. This is because the unconscious mind is vast. You can trust, though, that each time you do it, a layer of ego content in your unconscious mind has healed. Because of this, you will always get the ultimate effect of True Forgiveness: you will feel peaceful. Things which used to upset you don't even make a blip on your radar. Miracles truly are natural and they do await you. True Forgiveness transforms what you thought would break you into that which strengthens you. When you apply the correction of True Forgiveness at the level of cause, your mind, you will experience peaceful effects. It is the law.

Conclusion

*"You do not recognize the enormous waste of
energy you expend in denying the truth."*
~ T.9.I.11:1

M Y INTENTION with this book was to shine a much-needed light upon the mind and how it works. By now, you know that taking care of your mind is actually taking care of yourself, because you *are* Mind. Your mind's power is wasted when it is directed towards the ego's thought system of fear; as the Course suggests, this is an enormous waste of time. You can use your time more wisely and enjoy the loving experiences in your life while forgiving the ego content you find yourself reacting to. This is what time is for.

Lesson 44 of the Course instructs: *"Then try to sink into your mind, letting go every kind of interference and intrusion by quietly sinking past them.* **Your mind cannot be stopped in this unless you choose to stop it."** Too often I hear people say that 'meditation is difficult' and 'I can't shut my mind off!' I completely understand, but what I want to highlight is that a racing or unfocused mind is a choice. You are not a victim of your own mind – you rule your mind. Your mind's slipping into tangential issues is a choice and it's also a symptom of an untrained mind. With commitment and practice, your mind can be trained to focus with less distraction by the ego's ramblings. Remember, your belief in the ego makes it real to you. You *can* and inevitably will switch your allegiance to your Right Mind – this is how the ego will lose its potency.

"Do you not understand that to oppose the Holy Spirit is to fight yourself?" ~ T.30.II.1:1

The preface to the Course tells us that to be in the world of perception is to be caught in a dream which we cannot escape without help. Your Higher Self is that help. You have a choice between the ego and the Holy Spirit available to you at *all* times, as both are in your mind. You won't know the benefits of using your Right Mind until you put it into action. That's basic cause and effect. True Forgiveness and other teachings I have shared will be just words on a page until you implement them in your thinking and then begin to experience the loving effects of your Right Mind. Remember, your mind learns best through experience. You will only come to trust in your Higher Self through application of Right-Minded principles like non-judgement, True Forgiveness, True Denial and accepting the Atonement principle.

"You are at home in God, dreaming of exile but perfectly capable of awakening to reality." ~ T.10.I2:1

You will remember Who you really are. How quickly you return to the full awareness of your Reality is up to how often you turn to the Holy Spirit for support within the dream. You think you are a separate being, but your formless mind is actually perfectly connected to all things, including God. There is in fact only one mind. You don't see this formless Reality with your physical eyes, you experience it with your mind. Separation is not real despite what physical appearances may suggest. Everything is unified which the laws of the mind have shown. Now that you are aware of them, you can use them to your benefit. Your Source wills that you be happy and peaceful. Whenever you don't feel happy or peaceful, know that you have a thought to correct, not a fear to perpetuate. Your enlightenment begins with the correct use of your mind.

> *"What has been given you? The knowledge that you are a mind, in Mind and purely mind, sinless forever, wholly unafraid, because you were created out of love. Nor have you left your Source, remaining as you were created. This was given you as knowledge which you cannot lose. It was given as well to every living thing, for by that knowledge only does it live."*
> ~ Lesson 158.1:1-5

Acknowledgments

I would like to acknowledge my mentor, Dr. Tim Hall, who passed in early May of 2021. It was my dear hope he would have had an opportunity to read this book which was inspired by our work together. I know you are with me Tim, at the level of the mind. Thank you for the memories I will always have. Thank you also for your belief, your time, your unwavering support and also for your copy of *A Concordance of A Course in Miracles,* which you were happy to give me the second you learned I was a student of the Course.

I would also like to acknowledge my parents whose history has inspired the work I do. A child always watches, and I always noticed the hard work you put in to healing from the 'troubles' and embracing a new and happier life.

And, I would also like to acknowledge D. Patrick Miller. I always know my written work is in the best hands when I'm working with you. This is the second book we've worked together on and I know there's going to be many more! Thank you so dearly for your guidance.

Made in United States
Troutdale, OR
11/29/2023